PRAISE FOR HEALTHY CHURCH BY DESIGN

"There are many voices claiming to offer advice for building healthy Churches. Tim Songster's voice deserves to be heard. He brings to the table his vast experience in Church building construction coupled with his sincere faith in Christ to provide solid wisdom for ministries looking to make a difference for years to come."

Dr Rice Broocks
Author of God's Not Dead
Co-founder Every Nation Churches

"There is a divine connection between the call upon a church and the space they create to facilitate that purpose. Through years of experience, mixed with a call of God to serve the local church, Tim Songster taps into that connection. Through both practical and deeply spiritual insights, Tim will help you successfully step into the world of building and church construction. Tim's company, Cosco, built our present facility and a later addition. His construction expertise, mixed with his spiritual insights, made the process effective and life giving."

John Nuzzo
Senior Pastor
Victory Family Church

"Tim Songster nails it in *Healthy Church By Design* as he speaks real life into real church problems. Drawing from numerous years of experience ministering alongside churches and pastors, Tim, in his practical style, addresses the elephant in the room, 'When should a church build?'. I found his straightforward approach to be much needed and refreshing."

Dr. Steven L. Kyle
Lead Pastor
Hiland Park Baptist Church
Panama City, FL

"For any pastor who wants to have a balanced, faith-filled, intellectual, and strategic view of how God uses people and facilities to advance the gospel, this book by my dear friend Tim Songster will give you a True North to follow."

Pastor Tim Johnson
Orlando World Outreach Center

"So many people have written about church health and church growth. Yet it seems like the topic of church facilities and how they can help or hinder a church's ability to reach people for Christ has been neglected—until now. Tim Songster is an expert on this topic and has now written the book that will help church leadership do something about it."

Pastor Brian Boyles
FBC Snellville, GA

HEALTHY CHURCH BY DESIGN

The Synergy between Buildings and Church Health

Timothy A. Songster

Healthy Church by Design:
The Synergy between Buildings and Church Health

© 2018 by Timothy A. Songster
All rights reserved.

ISBN 978-1-948022-03-3
Rainer Publishing
www.RainerPublishing.com
Spring Hill, TN

Printed in the United States of America

Scripture quotations taken from the New American Standard Bible® (NASB), Copyright © 1960, 1962, 1963, 1968, 1971, 1972, 1973,1975, 1977, 1995 by The Lockman Foundation. Used by permission. www.Lockman.org

To Richard L. Songster, my brother, whom I lost in a tragic car accident on March 26, 1990. I look forward to seeing you in heaven.

CONTENTS

Foreword 11

Introduction 13

1. Defining Church Health 17

2. Synergy Between Buildings and Church Health 31

3. The Synergy of a Building and Evangelism 49

4. The Synergy of a Building and Fellowship 75

5. The Synergy of a Building and Discipleship 81

6. The Synergy of a Building and Worship 95

7. The Synergy of a Building and Ministry 103

8. The Synergy of a Building and Prayer 107

9. The Synergy of a Building and Outward Focus to Grow Healthier 111

10. Healthy Churches Versus Unhealthy Churches 117

11. Advice to Pastors and Leaders Entering a Building Program 127

12. Recommendations for Those Who Cannot Build Now ... 145

Acknowledgments 147

About the Author 149

End Notes 151

FOREWORD

Tim Songster knows churches.

The first time I met Tim, I was immediately impressed with his acumen and knowledge of church buildings. Concurrently, I was equally impressed with his design-build firm, Cosco & Associates, Inc. But the more I got to know him, the more I realized his scope of knowledge was well beyond the design and build of a church facility.

In a word, he knows churches.

Let me give you a real-life example. I was on the phone with a pastor where Tim had just made a presentation in his church. The pastor's church was considering constructing some new facilities, and so they asked Tim to make a presentation.

The pastor was blown away. Here is my best recollection of his words: "So I asked Tim to make a building presentation, but he and his team blew us away with all the other work they did. They had already visited our worship services. They knew a lot about our church's health. To say they went above and beyond is a massive understatement. They blew us away!"

Tim Songster indeed knows churches.

To put it mildly, this book arrives in my home with great anticipation. It is an incredible perspective of the healthy church from the perspective of a design-build firm, but it is much more. I serve thousands of churches through my blog, podcast, and subscription ministry, Church Answers. I can't wait to get this book in the hands of these leaders. I can wait for them to glean the practical insights and wisdom of Tim Songster.

This book is called *Healthy Church by Design*. It is a perfect title for the incredible content it contains. Indeed, I can see this book becoming an enduring part of every church leader's library for generations to come. It's just that good. It's the perfect marriage of church health and church facilities. It is a book so powerfully constructed that you will be left wishing you had it years ago.

So, when it's all said and done, you will agree with my thesis and perspective.

Tim Songster knows churches.

And after you have read *Healthy Church by Design*, you will know churches, including your own, so much better.

Thom S. Rainer
President and CEO, LifeWay Christian Resources
Author of *I Am a Church Member* and *The Welcoming Church*

INTRODUCTION

Growing up in a Christian home set the standard for loving Christ. Playing various sports from football, golf, track, swimming and diving, and wrestling gave me confidence in life. God showed me work ethic through swimming and diving, allowing me to excel and win many events, including the Empire State Games in Syracuse, New York, which then led to numerous scholarship opportunities. Because of my incredible respect for a godly father, I listened to his advice to take the challenge to go to the United States Air Force Academy in Colorado Springs as a member of their swimming and diving team. The Lord taught me character, discipline, integrity, and hard work at the USAF Academy.

As we learn in Proverbs, "Iron sharpens iron, so one man sharpens another" (27:17). I've been blessed to have great partners in the ministry who have shared incredible insight into various areas that affect ministry.

As the Lord taught me various areas of ministry, I felt like an athlete in training. I grew up in church, then was challenged to discover different Christian denominations and beliefs in order to further understand how various denominations interpret God's Word and apply it to their theologies and doctrines. I was blessed to be able to work in capital stewardship campaigns, Bible-based, money-management seminars, estate planning, financing, and architecture and construction. Before God called me to COSCO & Associates, I was ordained in ministry and began preaching the gospel. I've enjoyed being a Sunday school teacher, small group leader, care group leader, youth leader, deacon, usher, greeter, and preacher.

I've spent years studying every book I could find on church growth and church health, attending seminars about theories of church growth and health, and interviewing pastors and leaders of seemingly "healthy" churches. I have gleaned much from many successful and unsuccessful ministries. However, what I have not been able to discover is a book that clearly and simply explains how a facility or physical building can and will impact a church's health. That's what this book aims to do.

I hope this book will bless pastors, staff members, and lay leaders who are considering renovating or adding on to their churches. This book will address how church health is affected by building the right facility and how it is hindered by having a poor facility that stagnates healthy growth potential. This book will help pastors better define what to do in their current church facilities, and it is a resource they give to church leadership, staff members, and building team members to understand the "why" and the "wins" for building and renovating space.

Let them see You in me, Lord.

1 DEFINING CHURCH HEALTH

There are numerous definitions of what it means to be a healthy church. Having worked with hundreds of incredible ministries of various denominations, sizes, and demographics, I have been blessed with a unique perspective. As a servant of Jesus Christ, I want the church to grow stronger in its love for God, its understanding and application of God's Word, and its ministries of reaching, growing, and serving others.

Before addressing the correlation between a building and church health, let's define a healthy church.

Large worship attendance does not in itself signify a healthy church. I know of many numerically large churches that are far from what I consider biblically healthy. Instead, many of these churches are more of a country club with little to no biblical training, preaching of the entire counsel of the Word of God, or spiritual and personal growth. Unfortunately, many of those churches are producing watered-down, milk-toast Christians whose ears are tickled and easily "tossed here and there" by false doctrine (Ephesians 4:14). Likewise, an obsession with size and growth has set up a generation of pastors who feel they are failing because they are not growing to mega-church size. The focus on weekend attendance leaves many pastors and church members feeling either proud or discouraged.

God did create everything to grow. The communities around us need Christ, and we need to be expanding God's kingdom. However, each church has its own unique DNA, gifting, and potential. The real question is, "Are our priorities in order?" Our priorities should be to accomplish the purposes of God, people, programs, and then property. We need to be praying for God's Spirit to move in our churches and be willing to become the people and places God can use for His work.

God has gifted each of us with different talents, harvests, and soil conditions. The best focus is on the quality of work and faithfulness to what God has called each of us. Our reward will be hearing those words, "Well done, good and faithful slave" (Matthew 25:21). At the judgment seat of Christ, He will ask, "What did you do with what I gave you?" First Corinthians says, "For we are God's fellow workers; you are God's field, God's building. According to the grace of God which was given to me, like a wise master builder I laid a foundation, and another is building on it. But each man must be careful how he builds on it. For no man can lay a foundation other than the one which is laid, which is Jesus Christ . . . Each man's work will become evident; for the day will show it because it is *to be* revealed with fire, and the fire itself will test the quality of each man's work" (3:9–11, 13, emphasis added). We are all called to build the church through faithful ministry.

Sometimes plateaued or declining growth happens because God is not currently calling people in that particular area. Most of the time, however, the reason is that the congregation is still working through its own internal problems and is not ready for an influx of new believers and would not assimilate them properly. If we are not willing to let God work in us and through us, He will work elsewhere.

There are many reasons churches today are not healthy including incorrect expectations, a lack of a clear discipleship process, inward focus, poor leadership and people skills, and moral failures. However, I believe the primary reason churches today are not healthy and being revitalized is the lack of God's presence. When your church has a worship service, can you authentically say that one will encounter God's presence? Encountering God changes a person, and nothing else matters. I have been in some of the worst buildings and experienced the presence of God. Likewise, I've been in some of the most beautiful buildings where I experienced incredible music, speaking, drama, and friendly people, but I did not encounter God and therefore left unchanged. The key to a healthy and revitalized church is encountering the presence of God. Nothing except our Lord Jesus will change us.

Currently in the United States, I have mostly experienced churches that have largely sold out to entertainment or an experience rather than God's presence. Many people have found this entertainment system lacking. People are starving for an authentic God experience. They want God—not a "good service"—as the primary focus of the church.

I dream of walking into a church full of tremendous love like I've never witnessed before. That is supposed to be our apologetic. John 13:35 tells us that "all men will know that you are My disciples, if you have love by one another." Scripture tells us that this love is supposed to convince the world. Third John 1:6 explains that even strangers will testify of our love, hospitality, and kindness before the church. I want to walk into a church where the person praying up front actually looks like he is talking to a holy God and is connected and honored to come into His presence. I want to be under a leader who is not just a great speaker but who knows God deeply and causes others to desire that kind of personal relationship with a holy God. A leader is someone whose life displays that he authentically lives for Christ, shares the gospel, and walks closely with Christ. You see it in his marriage, in his children, in his work, and in his daily life.

I desire a church where the people hunger for holiness, confessing and repenting instead of merely trying to relieve guilt or seeing how much sin they can get away with and still go to heaven. I yearn for a church that is filled with people longing for holiness, where the people are on a mission to share the gospel message to the ends of the earth. The people have a compassion for the poor that Jesus spoke about. They have abundant personal relationships with God outside of Sundays. They walk into the worship service, and it is evident they had serious time alone with God during the previous week and now are coming together to celebrate.

I dream of a church where the members believe they have received gifts from the Spirit and that those spiritual manifestations enable them to build others up and are used for the common good. The attitude of the people is, "Whom can I serve today?" and "Whom can I build up today?" The church is a place where there is evidence of the supernatural. Someone once said that the problem with today's church is that it is neither *super* nor *natural*. A person may think that he or she doesn't see anything unusual in many churches—that the churches appear to be just like the world. So much of our church may appear forced, timed, and manipulated. I long for a church where there is a sense of awe, as if I gathered with these zealous people who are filled with something I have never seen before.

When you experience God like this in His church, then we are doing a great work.

To accomplish this, the church pastoral staff must first seek the Lord's face, be in the Word, and pray for revival in their hearts. Only then will the church lay leadership follow toward encountering God in a fresh and heartfelt way. Then the congregation will follow their lead to seek the presence of God. After we get this right, the rest of the material I am going to share will make our ministry that much more effective.

My definition of a healthy church is when it is evangelizing the lost, discipling the saved, and moving the disciples into serving in ministry. The church will continue to be revitalized by staying outwardly focused, serving, loving, and giving to the surrounding community, and connecting to Christ. A healthy pastoral staff authentically places Jesus as their life (Colossians 3:4), understands that serving is a blessing and an honor, and remains in Him. A healthy church member understands he is the salt and light to the community, called to be Christ to others wherever God has him/her (leading, teaching, and training families in the faith), and to love, give, and serve others in the name of Jesus Christ.

A healthy church is about relationships: man to God and man to man. God created us for both.

Pastor Rick Warren stated in his article, "Forget Church Growth, Aim for Church Health," that "The purposes of the church are commanded by Jesus in the Great Commandment and Great Commission, further explained by Paul in Ephesians 4, described in Jesus' prayer for the church in John 17, and modeled by the first church in Jerusalem."[1]

Warren further explains the healthy church using Acts 2:42–47 as a guide:

> They were continually devoting themselves to the apostles' teaching and to fellowship, to the breaking of bread and to prayer. Everyone kept feeling a sense of awe; and many wonders and signs were taking place throughout the apostles. And all those who had believed were together and had all things in common; and they began selling their property and possessions and were sharing them with all, as anyone might have need. Day by day continuing with one mind in the temple, and breaking bread from house to house, they were taking their meals together with gladness and sincerity of heart, praising God and having favor with all the people. And the Lord was adding to their number day by day those who were being saved.[2]

Don't miss that it was the Lord who was adding to their numbers and saving the lost. The reason God was able to move the way He did was mainly because God's people were acting as a healthy church. If the church is doing the right things, according to Scripture, then the only limitation to growing is not having the correct tools to use. We will cover these concepts in the coming chapters.

Acts 2 mentions many facets of church health:

- They were devoted to studying God's Word and the apostles' teaching.
- They were in fellowship by partnering, connecting, and sharing with one another.
- They took communion together.
- They were in prayer individually and corporately.
- They were edifying each other and meeting each other's needs.
- They were worshiping together.
- They were ministering to the needy.
- They were evangelizing the lost.

As a result, verse 47 says, "And the Lord was adding to their number day by day those who were being saved."

God gave us the seven guiding principles of a healthy church:

1. Churches grow larger through evangelism.
2. Churches grow warmer through fellowship.
3. Churches grow deeper through discipleship.
4. Churches grow stronger through worship.
5. Churches grow broader through ministry.
6. Churches grow closer through prayer.
7. Churches grow healthier through staying outwardly focused.[3]

Scripture confirms that the purposes of a biblically healthy church include evangelism, discipleship, fellowship, ministry, worship, prayer, and outward focus. After helping a person understand the gospel and God calling him or her into salvation, the church must teach a new Christian how to love God and worship Him, connect with other believers, study God's Word, and grow in understanding of who God is and how to live for Him alone. Small groups (such as Sunday school groups, community groups, connect groups—churches have different labels for such groups) also teach believers how to grow in their relationship with Christ and how to serve, read His Word, pray, and continue growing in their faith. The healthy church teaches its people to understand their spiritual giftings and use them to serve the Lord in ministry. Church members learn how to serve Christ by loving others and giving of themselves in order to bring honor and glory to Him. I have observed that healthy churches are effective first at equipping (Eph. 4:11-12), then empowering people to grow into the men and women God has called them to be by encouraging movement from worship, to small groups and connecting with other believers, to serving the Lord in ministry. A healthy church has an outward focus in budget, programming, and action. They are in the community loving, serving, and giving with a Christlike heart to meet needs.

Rick Warren states that "church growth is the natural result of church health."[4] Warren Wiersbe believes that "there needs to be one more Beatitude: Blessed are the balanced."[5]

The key word for church health is balance. A healthy church is balanced in purpose between evangelism, fellowship, discipleship, worship, ministry, prayer, and outward focus.

Each purpose of the church must be in equilibrium with the others for health to occur. Likewise, our facilities must be in equilibrium. A good facility is simply a ministry tool that will enable ministry to be done well, but an inadequate tool can also hinder ministry. When it comes to your church building, what limits your church growth is whatever is inadequate. A church will only grow to the limit of its weakest element, such as parking, worship space, small groups, relational or connection space, and preschool and children space. The most successful building project will provide every demographic a win, and the "why" of the space will be communicated effectively to your members. Unless you seek an intentional balance between the seven purposes, your church will tend to overemphasize the purpose that best expresses the gifts and passion of its pastor or leaders, causing the ministry to be out of balance and ineffective.

Pursuing church health principles instead of only church growth principles allows us to focus on the legitimate desire to see the church flourish without some of the impure motivations that might trip us up. As we pursue church health, church growth will likely also occur.

Rick Warren hit the nail on the head when he stated: "What then is the secret of church health? In a word—it's balance!"[6] I could not agree more, as this book will bear out. When our body systems are in balance, we are healthy. When our bodies get out of balance, we have sickness and disease. Likewise, when the body of Christ—and church facilities—becomes unbalanced, disease occurs.[7]

Healthy growth is achieved through the right balance of ministry, enhanced with the correct facilities, and not infected by the wrong facilities. To revitalize a church and remain healthy, we must restore balance to the body, soul, and congregation with a matching facility. It begins with God moving and reviving the hearts of His people to have a balanced approach to ministry. It is enhanced by the balance (or hindered by the lack of balance) of the facilities.

Thom Rainer's book, *I Am a Church Member*, reminds us of the aspects of biblical church membership, which greatly impact the culture and health of our ministry.[8] Each church would benefit and be blessed beyond what we can even imagine if all of our people understood these simple, profound principles of what it means to be healthy church members. Instead of having an entitlement mentality, we are reminded that the Bible calls us to serve, care, pray, learn, teach, and give abundantly and without hesitation to others.

We learn that biblical church members give without qualification and view tithes and offerings as joyous. They become a unifying presence in the church. They actually give up their preferences when they join. They are committed to serve others and Christ. They pray for their church leadership. They take responsibility for encouraging and leading their families to worship together in church. They treasure membership as a gift.[9]

Gratefully, there are numerous excellent books in the Christian world about how to grow a healthy church and what a healthy church does. Thom Rainer's research in *Autopsy of a Deceased Church* provides statistical data behind what factors in churches in America are separating the healthy churches (statistically about 30 percent) from others that are sick, very sick, or dying. One of the common factors of a sick, a very sick, and a dying church is an inward focus verses outward focus.[10]

Many of us in ministry understand that church health is the key to church growth. All living things grow if they're healthy. Anything that does not grow is unhealthy. You don't have to make living organisms grow—it's natural for them to do so. I did not have to force my two boys to grow. They naturally grew up. As long as I removed the hindrances, such as poor nutrition, disease, or an unsafe environment, their growth was automatic.

So is church health and growth the same? The answer, I believe, is no. Of course, a healthy church will grow; healthy growth is non-negotiable. The world needs it, God commands it, and we should all experience it. If a church is healthy, then by default it will grow numerically, spiritually, and in influence. I have never experienced a church that was healthy that did not grow. A better question might be: "Does the church want to do what it takes to become all that God has called it to be to reach this world for Christ?"

Further, church growth potential resides in many factors. Churches are limited by their locations, their giftings, and their commitment levels to Christ. The fact remains that there are lost people in every church community who desperately need Christ. It is our mandate to reach them. While I agree that not all churches are called to be megachurches (similar to the parable of talents), all churches are called to reach the lost and disciple the saved. We cannot make excuses for not reaching our potential in Christ, personally or corporately. All churches are called to minister to the community, to be salt and light. If a church is not reaching people and changing lives, the church is not effective or obedient.

2 SYNERGY BETWEEN BUILDINGS AND CHURCH HEALTH

There is a natural synergy between your building and the health of your church. Healthy churches have facilities that are well cared for, clean, and usable. The members see their building as a gathering point and tool for use by God and His people. Likewise, members of healthy churches that rent a meeting space treat it with respect and keep it maintained and clean, seeing it as a form of evangelism.

In contrast, unhealthy churches tend to have facilities that may be well cared for and clean, but they tend not to be usable; the members see their church as a ministry to itself and not to be messed up. This often keeps part of the facility from being used, especially for community events. Churches where the facilities are dilapidated, dirty, and unsanitary tend to be that way in worship and ministry. Likewise, members of unhealthy churches that rent do not treat their rented building with respect; they often have an us-versus-them mentality.

After working with hundreds of ministries of various denominations, demographics, and areas of the country, it has become apparent that there are underlying traits when a facility directly impacts the church's health as a whole.

The correct facility can greatly impact the potential for healthy church growth. Likewise, an incorrect facility can largely stagnate the growth of a church. If the church doesn't take care of what we have, we are not being good stewards of what God has given us. In addition, it sends the wrong message to visitors and guests. If we understand that, then it will change how we feel about our facilities—since none of us want our facilities to become a barrier to reaching our communities.

Let me emphasize that I do not believe the blanket statement, "If you build it, they will come." With the best intentions in mind, a church may decide to build with hopes that it will attract more people; however, it may put the ministry in more undue stress with a financial burden that will not allow them to minister effectively. There is a time to build. You build when your ministry is growing and out of space or when your facility is so dilapidated that it is hindering growth and you have a financial strategy to pay for it with your current cash flow. You build when your church is healthy and vibrant, not when it is broken and sick. From years of experience, I know that any issue that exists in the church will be exposed and magnified by a building program.

Building the right building in faith will also bless the church and stretch its faith. The choices you make in designing and using your building will directly affect your church's growth potential. It affects the flow of people, security, flexibility and adaptability of space, as well as usability of the size of spaces to match occupancy and capacity. The resulting space, good or bad, will directly affect the culture of your building tool. You will define your building, then your building will define you. The choices you make and the care you take of your facility is affected by your decisions. The results of those decisions affect how well the space can be used for ministry and will limit or expand your potential.

In the book of Haggai we learn about the Jews returning to Jerusalem after being exiled. Their first step was to build the temple, the house of God. After they began, they stopped working on the temple and began working on their own homes for their own benefits. They neglected the house of God for ten years.

Many of our churches today are also neglected, but church goers have beautiful new homes and cars, go on exotic vacations, etc. This is not to insinuate that nice things are sinful, but neglecting the church for unnecessary luxuries is out of order. (By the way, if all church members tithed according to biblical standards, the church would have all the money it would need to do ministry and to build and update its buildings.)

God wanted to understand why the returning Jews had neglected the temple and not noticed its decline. "The Lord of Hosts says this: These people say: The time has not come for the house of the Lord to be rebuilt . . . Is it a time for you yourselves to live in your paneled houses, while this house lies in ruins?" (Haggai 1:2–4 HCSB).

God was not happy that His house was in ruins: "When you brought the harvest to your house, I ruined it. Why? . . . Because My house still lies in ruins, while each of you is busy with his own house" (1:9 HCSB).

In the books of Ezra and Nehemiah, the Israelites returned after seventy years of Babylonian captivity to Jerusalem to rebuild the temple and the walls of Jerusalem. Through this passage, God gives another great example of how to trust Him and His provision when He tells us to revitalize His church facility or build His church. This shows us how to honor and trust Him when we come up against resistance and how to defeat the enemy.

Nehemiah 4:14 says, "When I saw their fear, I rose and spoke to the nobles, to the officials, to the rest of the people. 'Do not be afraid of them; remember the Lord who is great and awesome, and fight for your brothers and your sons, your daughters, your wives, and your houses' . . . Our God will fight for us" (4:14, 20 NASB). So Nehemiah urged the people to complete the wall. What happened? "When all our enemies heard of it, and all the nations surrounding us saw it, they lost their confidence; for they recognized that this work had been accomplished with the help of God" (6:16 NASB).

The Lord showed us that throughout this process of building, renovating, or expanding, there will be challenges and challengers. However, He also showed us that we can trust Him, stand firm, and glorify Him.

You may also ask yourself, Why build for those yet to come? Paul told the church in Philippians 2:1–4: "If then there is any encouragement in Christ, if any consolation of love, if any fellowship of the Spirit, if any affection and mercy, fulfill my joy by thinking the same way, having the same love, sharing the same feelings, focusing on one goal. Do nothing out of rivalry or conceit, but in humility consider others as more important than yourselves. Everyone should look out not only for his own interests, but also for the interest of others" (HCSB). It is critical that believers continue to think about not only discipling the saved but also preparing to reach those who have yet to come into our churches. We must have facilities that attract people to, not distract them from, the gospel.

Thom Rainer made a clear comparison that sums up the idea of reaching others and preparing for those yet to come:

"Other First = Life. Me First = Death." His study explains that members of a dying church had the common trait of being unwilling to go into the community to reach and minister to people. They weren't willing to invite their unchurched friends and relatives or expend the funds necessary for a vibrant outreach. Even if the church began to grow, the members of the dying church would only accept the growth if the new members were like them and if the church would continue to "do church" the way they wanted it, that is, if the growth met their preferences and allowed them to remain comfortable.[11]

FACILITY BALANCE

Let's begin by looking at the overall campus. If we were to get into a helicopter and look down at the ideal campus, it would look like the following diagram. I first heard of this concept at a men's conference from a sharp man, Mr. Alan Taylor, who was that the time serving at First Baptist Woodstock.

Seldom does a church get an opportunity to relocate and start over with a new piece of property. Most churches start with the footprints they have, with hope they can adjust the adjacencies and reuse existing facilities by adding to or replacing them. These principles still apply in those

SYNERGY BETWEEN BUILDINGS AND CHURCH HEALTH / 37

You never have a second chance to make a first impression.

Facilities should look someone cares. Clean up the clutter.

Facilities should look like we are expecting company.

FACILITY MASTER PLANNING

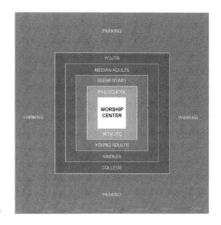

instances. A church campus will be a much more effective tool if we have the adjacencies of space correct in order to make attending a great experience.

A great experience for all attendees begins with parking. (Think about how many guests turn around and go home because the parking lot was confusing or they couldn't find an available spot.) Parking should be adjacent to each side, as close to each building and ministry space as possible.

Everything should develop around the worship experience. Therefore, if we were to start with a fresh site, the worship center should be the hub of the campus. This area should be supplemented with properly sized common areas or a large lobby space with seating groups, welcome center, cafe, media center, restrooms, guest reception, information centers, etc., in order to create a culture where people can connect and relate. Ideally, the space should be kept simple and directions to other spaces (children's ministry, worship center, etc.) so that visiting families can easily determine where to go.

Closest to the worship center should be the senior adult small group spaces. Senior adults cannot get around as easily as teenagers, so making a senior adult travel to another floor or across campus does not express care for senior adults. Senior parking and some handicap spaces should also be close to the facility.

Equally important for a balanced facility is the nursery/preschool space. Having a young family carry diaper bags, strollers, car seats, touting babies, toddlers, and preschoolers across campus, up or down stairs, is simply inconsiderate. It is necessary to provide parking for young mothers close to the entrance and the preschool drop-off area. Ideally, the nursery/preschool area should have a secured drop off, with safety check-in and check-out procedures in place, so that parents can know their children are safe and secure while in worship and small groups. Also, providing soft play for toddlers with a clean and uncluttered space, including vibrant colors at the reception area, says to the parents, "We care about children." Quality facilities with the proper emphasis put the parents at ease and project that you are not just babysitting children—you are caring, teaching, and ministering to them.

As you move farther away from the worship center, you ideally have the elementary children. This space would also benefit from cleanliness, vibrant colors, and security check-in and check-out procedures. An indoor play facility that is highly visible from the common area indicates that children are important to the church. Locating the drop-off area close to the preschool area is practical. As preschoolers grow into children, and their younger brothers or sisters are still in preschool, it is comforting to have them in a similar area. Unfortunately, many campuses send parents on a hike throughout the campus to drop off and pick up children.

It also is wise to have the young adults' small group space near the worship center and their children. It saves time and allows young families to assimilate, relate, connect, and encourage one another to move from worship into small groups and serving.

As you move farther away, adult, singles, and college ministry small group space make sense. Generally speaking, the distance for these groups of people to travel to these spaces is not a distraction or discouragement. Ideally, the campus should provide good people flow and directional signage from the street to the seat. A hub, or common area, for connecting spaces and moving people will provide for simplicity and relationship building.

Lastly, youth space can be the farthest from the hub.

This does not diminish the importance or the need for quality space. Generally speaking, this group is the most flexible and will adapt to any space as long as they can claim it and make it their own. Security and supervision remains critical, even though they are young adults. Let them use their creativity to create a space where they can connect, worship, and learn. Providing a quality experience with activities that they cannot potentially get at home is key. For example, today's teens have games on their smartphones and PlayStations or Xboxes at home. Pool tables, ping-pong, foosball, four-square, and nine-square are things they can do together, enjoy, and don't usually have at home.

Note that every demographic should have ADA accessibility.

THE PROCESS OF DISCOVERY

Over the years of working with churches, we have refined a process that will help you discover what facility needs you have and will provide you with the best tools for ministry. The first thing to understand is that it is a process, not an event. It takes time to assess where you are, what you have, and what you need to take your ministry to the next level of church health.

As professionals, we begin this process by worshiping

with the ministry. Even though we only design and build church facilities and it's our passion, business, and ministry to do so, this process is critical for us to understand what is happening in your ministry and how God has uniquely equipped you to reach your community. There is an opportunity to evaluate first impressions of your ministry and give quality feedback as to how your ministry can improve outside of renovation or building a new facility.

To further understand your ministry DNA and your church culture, I recommend meeting with each ministry team in the church. Each meeting should include the ministry staff member responsible for each area as well as key lay-leaders involved. This process may take several days since at least forty-five minutes is needed with each team. This process will discover what your team thinks are the good, the bad, and the ugly of each ministry. You will discover various ministry leaders' God-given visions for their areas of ministry. It will further allow you to discover how well your vision has been captured throughout your ministries. As a pastor, you will hear things that are both refreshing and surprising. You will have an opportunity to make adjustments and correct any sickness, such as disunity, that exists.

I further recommend a study of your community demographics and psychographics. First, understand what is defined as your community that you minister to and draw from (this could be a radius of distance or zip codes). I recommend using a service such as The Percept Group to evaluate the statistical characteristics of the human population (demographics) and the characteristics of the human population within a human population according to their attitudes, aspirations, etc. (pyschographics). This will provide you with "who" are your prospects as well as "what they think."

It is also helpful to ask a guest to visit your services once every six months and evaluate your facility using a short survey. This survey should evlaluate the first impressions of the website, the building, the worship experience, and ministries, including first impression areas explained in Chapter 3. ThomRainer.com has a great example of a secret guest survey that you can follow. You can encourage a visitor to fill this out with an incentive such as a gift card to a local restaurant. This will provide valuable feedback as to how you are doing as a ministry from a visitor's perspective. We will talk more about this in the next chapter.

After this, your leadership team needs to review first impressions and ministry team meeting notes to begin the process of prioritizing the existing needs. The priority should be focusing on providing tools that will lead to health in each ministry.

Next, you need to assess the financial health of your ministry. This is probably the most difficult and most overlooked part of the process. I will cover the basics, but this is certainly not enough to fully understand its impact on a project and your ministry. Most churches do not fully understand their financial position or how it correlates to the potential to renovate or add buildings to improve their tools and fix deficiencies or hindrances to church growth. Financial health and church health are directly related to each other. A financially healthy church has members who are generous and understand the lordship of Christ over finances. They give abundantly with a cheerful heart and without strings attached. It is the responsibility, in the name of good stewardship, of the church leaders to learn outward focus in budgeting, as well as how to budget each ministry. If you have a ministry that is thriving, it is probably well funded. On the other hand, if a ministry is failing, you may need to evaluate if that ministry lines up with the core values of the church. If it passed that test, you may need to invest funding to revitalize it. For example, your church may have an older demographic that is reaching few young families because the preschool and children facilities are dated, unsafe, and unclean. Have families left because you were not prepared to take care of them? You may need to consider revitalizing those areas to attract young families who are willing to put their children in that space.

As far as tithes and offerings, follow the money. Scripture

tells us that where your heart is, there will be your treasure also. If you see where your people respond, what ministry offerings are highly funded, then you will know the heart of the people and the church. Ask yourself which areas of ministry are uniquely strong, which areas your people most participate in and volunteer to help. These areas are likely well-funded.

After deciding a ministry direction and understanding your financial position, develop a fiscal plan that will allow you to take on the building project without financial hardship. To do so, first study your current giving trends and cash flow. Your giving culture will not change just because you are entering a building program. If you have a problem with your congregation giving, perhaps educating and training your members regarding the importance of stewardship is necessary. To change your capacity, you must first change your giving culture. If your capital campaign is not handled properly, and potentially even when it is handled properly, the general budget could slightly decrease for a period of time as members give to a building campaign. The net result is still much improved, but unfortunately some members don't remember or realize that a tithe is different from an offering. Most well-handled, Spirit-led campaigns will result in an increased awareness of stewardship, and both your general budget (tithes) and building campaign (offerings) will increase.

How much money you can raise is based on several factors:

- the type of facility you are building;
- the professional you use;
- the current giving culture;
- large-donor development.
- follow up and follow through;
- involvement of a high percentage of your people serving in the campaign (over 70%)

A proper, Spirit-led capital campaign and training on stewardship should unify the church, communicate the heart of the ministry, and increase giving.

It is wise to have a plan for debt service for the building project that would build the cash flow into your current operating budget over the coming years so that you can handle the building project without depending on only fundraising or losing the ability to do ministry. Consider beginning to put the amount of debt service you plan on handling into a savings account to ensure that it does not hinder your ability to do ministry. If you cannot continue to do ministry with excellence and make that payment into savings, it is likely you won't be able to do ministry with excellence and pay a lender. Furthermore, your operating budget should include an amount for future building renovations and maintenance. As our buidings get older, we must plan for expeditures to update and repair them.

Here is a formula I recommend for setting a project budget for a building program:

> Project budget = Cash on Hand + Safe Debt Limit − Existing Debt + 80% of Capital Campaign Commitments + God's Leading

A safe debt limit in the above formula is taken from several factors. It is a calculation based on the annual receipts over the previous three years, the number of giving units in the church, the number of commitments made in a capital campaign, and the debt service available in the operating budget. For example, let's say a church has $250,000 of debt, $500,000 of cash on hand outside of an operating budget emergency fund (I recommend three months of operating budget), $1,000,000 pledged over the next three years in their capital campaign, and a safe debt limit of $2,500,000. Based on this information, I would set the entire project budget at $3,550,000. The final numbers must be bathed in prayer, and then we allow the peace of God to rule.

You should develop a plan that will allow you to pay off the debt you encounter in a building program in the next ten years to fifteen years maximum. It's been my experience that when a church builds the right building tool, at the right time, in the right location, and for the right reasons, it will experience 30 percent growth in attendance the first year. This will later translate to increased giving if the new growth is assimilated properly. It has also been my experience that although a current congregation will make the project happen, with proper health and the right tools, the additional new members will pay for the new building. If, for example, your growth increased by 30 percent followed by a 30 percent increase in revenue, that usually covers the majority of the debt service from your building program if sized properly.

Building a new building isn't merely for current members. Members build a new building or renovate an existing structure to provide space and a tool to reach, disciple, and minister to more people.

Spiritual renewal won't happen by acquiring a permanent building. It will happen through prayer and proclamation of the Word of God. By stepping out on a faith journey led by God, what the church will get out of a building project is greater than the building itself. God matures us in our faith through extra giving, sacrifice, and being a part of something greater than we are. This unique opportunity will give church members an opportunity to impact the future.

3

THE SYNERGY OF A BUILDING AND EVANGELISM

How can our facility help us share the gospel and reach people for Christ? There is a synergy of a building and evangelism that will help you grow larger. This begins with having the correct first impressions.

From the street to the seat, the church building makes a statement to any potential visitors. Visitors, whether consciously or subconsciously, compare your space to how they take care of their homes, maintain their own landscaping, and take care of their children. If our impression is negative, then a visitor may ask, "Can I trust this church with my child?" or "Can I trust this church with my family's spiritual health?"

By definition, evangelism is the spreading of the Christian gospel by public preaching or personal witness. It is the practice of relaying information about God to others with the intention of conversion.

Evangelism has often been called overflow. In other words, evangelism results from being so filled with the love of God and the joy of His salvation that it simply bubbles out or overflows from us.

It is no surprise that this usually can't happen during a time when we are still struggling to cope with past hurts, relationship problems, and a sense of loss. While we are in a grieving process, it is difficult to reach out to others. During such a time, we are still in need of nurture ourselves. It is also apparent that effective evangelism can't happen if we are not on fire for Jesus Christ in our private lives.

If most of the congregation is lukewarm or struggling in their personal relationship with Jesus, then the first need is prayer for the spiritual renewal of the congregation.

A great worship experience combined with a great building makes us want to invite others to our church, to talk about our excitement for our children's facilities, etc., as we interact with people. If you are embarrassed or lukewarm about your church and its buildings, you are not likely to invite others to experience it. The same principle is true of our homes. We are not quick to invite others over if there are dirty clothes lying about or dust bunnies rolling around.

I will never forget the first weekend of services at Victory

Family Church in Cranberry, Pennsylvania. The church opened its newly built worship center with an incredible commons area, including many relational spaces, seating groups, coffee cafe, and incredible preschool, children, and youth facilities. The worship was incredible, and the preaching was awesome. But what I remember most is the first impressions. When I arrived on campus a hospitality ministry team directed traffic, guided me to the building, and greeted me with a "Good morning! We are glad you're here!" When I got to the door, more people welcomed me with smiles. The building was clean and uncluttered. It looked like they were expecting company. There were people stationed everywhere on campus with tall signs with "Ask Me" on them to help direct visitors. Signage was easily visible from every entrance and throughout the campus. Security was in the parking lot and in the building. I walked in the building and quickly knew where to go. The restrooms were evenly spread throughout the campus and were clean, beautiful, and more than adequate. A welcome center with information was easily identifiable. Children and preschool spaces were well secured. The worship began with a countdown to service, both in the commons with digital signage and in the worship center. The worship was done with excellence. I was ushered into the presence of God. The welcome was personal and friendly; announcements and information were professional and understandable. The message was well delivered and scripturally based. The giving was done with an explanation of a "giving talk," and I was put at ease and understood what was happening. The closing was outstanding.

Imagine how you would feel about your church with this excellence that allowed God to work. The best part of this story is that this very weekend alone, over 128 people gave their lives to Christ. Awesome!

The largest impact a facility can make on reaching people for Christ is the first impression. Remember, you never get a second chance to make a first impression. The facility must represent open arms welcoming visitors and directing them to a strong entry point. It is true that guests will make a decision on whether or not they are coming back to the church again in the first five to seven minutes. These first minutes of experience are critical. A guest should receive more than five touches before they get into their seat in the worship center.

People drive by your facility every day and devise a perception of what your church is, the type of people who go there, and whether they would fit in. If we can break down those barriers, we can get them to come and see Jesus. Like our homes, our facilities reflect us. Potential visitors ask themselves: Do they care about children? Are my kids going to be safe? Do they care about their facility? Is the facility clean? Will I be comfortable? Will I be welcomed? A healthy church makes good first impressions and is designed to take care of its members as well as be outwardly focused.

One of the problems we face in maintaining our buildings is that we tend to overlook defects after one or two months. Once you become familiar with the building, you stop noticing what is wrong with it. The faded paint, dilapidated carpet, and holes in the parking lot become normal. Unfortunately, these things stand out immediately to visitors.

Pastor Matt Gates at Victory Family Church in Cranberry Township, Pennsylvania gave me a great analogy for first impressions. When a person comes onto your campus, they already have walls up in their lives. These walls may be to protect them from being hurt or to decide whether they want to be a part of your church family. As they are greeted in the parking lot by a hospitality ministry, then greeted at the door with a friendly smile, letting them know that you are glad they are here, the bricks on their wall begin to come down one at a time. Good signage and a good hospitality ministry allow them to know where they need to go in the building. Bricks come down. They stop in the warm, clean restroom. Bricks come down. They drop off their children at the clean and secure children ministry entrance, decorated with vivid colors and full of friendly people. The bricks come down. Then they move to the worship center and experience pleasant music playing and are greeted by more friendly people. The bricks come down. They experience great worship and bricks come down. Then, when the pastor brings God's Word, rightly divided, the walls are down and they are ready to receive. First impressions work hard at bringing the walls down and inviting guests with open arms to be a part of this church family.

Whether we like it or not, our facilities reflect our ministries. Have we neglected them? Do they look like we are expecting company? Have we cleaned up the clutter and provided an environment where worship and study are not hindered by physical barriers?

We learn of the paraplegic who was brought to Jesus in Mark 2:1–5. The church decided they were going to do whatever it took to get him to Jesus, the Son of God. It took a team to get him to Jesus—they had to tear open a roof and lower the man in from above. Then they trusted Jesus to do His part. This presents us with several questions:

- Are we willing to tear open our roofs (or any part of our facilities) in order to get a person to Jesus and be healed?
- Are we willing to work as a team to get the sick into our buildings to see Jesus?

- Do the sick see a reflection of Christ in us and in our facilities, or do the facilities say that we just don't care that much?
- Are our homes more important than our church homes?

Think about the interior and the exterior of any national chain store in your area. The average retail businesses will remodel their facilities every four to seven years, and with good reason. All you need to do is observe your local McDonalds, Burger King, or Taco Bell to see the constant change. You see it with companies rebranding themselves and constantly coming out with the "new and improved" products to make your life easier and happier. There's something about new that attracts. By contrast, most churches renovate their facilities every twenty-five to forty years, and some go until the local jurisdiction makes them update it to code or the facility fails structurally.

If your church building is more than fifteen to twenty years old, it is probably a growth-restricting obstacle. This does not mean that the Lord cannot work in your ministry; however, it does mean that you have created barriers to growth and ministry.

Before a visitor hears a sermon or gets into a small group, the first impression of your ministry is the parking lot, landscaping, and the building. Visitors first see the outside, then the inside. Visitors don't need to be professional architects to understand that the sidewalks are crumbling, the ceiling is too low, the halls are too narrow, the carpet is worn out, the seats are uncomfortable, or the color schemes are from a different generation. As Marshall McLuhan once said, "The medium is the message."[18] And your building is your medium. Your ministry defines the building, then your building defines your ministry.

The aesthetics of your church have a much bigger influence on your visitors than your regular attendees. Why? Members, although inconvenienced and annoyed at times, are used to the facility. The longer a person is at your church, the less he or she is able to see the building through the eyes of a newcomer. Members don't notice the water-stained marks in the ceiling tile, the chipped paint corners on the wall, or the worn-out carpet. Those things don't really matter to long-time attendees because they are coming for the people, the relationships, the fellowship, the spiritual growth. But for visitors with none of these reasons to attend, other things shape their first impression—and your building is one of them.

PARKING FIRST IMPRESSION

When you drive onto the church campus, there should be no question where you need to go. The campus should look welcoming. Many of us have experienced church campuses that are uninviting and hard to navigate. An adequate parking lot should have quality, tall signage that is easily visible and directs newcomers to visitor parking, young mother parking, and handicap parking is, as well the entrance, the worship center, the nursery, etc. Parking signage must be tall and large enough with proper font size to read quickly in a moving vehicle, with other vehicles in the parking lot. Signage painted on the ashalt or concrete pavement is not easily visible with any traffic.

Guest/Visitor parking should be the best parking, closest to the main entrance, and easy to find. Include an adequate amount of parking spaces, as if you are expecting a large number of visitors each week. Make visitors feel like important and distinguished guests. Consider providing guest parking with a sign labeled "guest parking for first 2-3 visits". This is an intentional encouragement for a return visit..

For a larger campus, have signage at your main entrances that asks visitors to turn on their hazard lights. This will allow your hospitality team to direct them immediately to the visitor parking and give them VIP treatment.

It could read, "First Time Guests: Turn on Hazard Lights for Parking Assistance."

You should also leave the best parking open for the elderly, handicapped, and new mothers. These parking spaces should also be close to the main entrances. The buildings should include at least one drive-under drop-off space for inclement weather or people needing assistance. Teach your leaders and staff to take worst parking first. Remind members to not park in guest parking.

Consider and protect drive routes around busy areas and crosswalks. You may need to post active control (people involved in this ministry or paid policemen) when necessary. Your members and guests will appreciate the attention to safety.

Consider a parking ministry or hospitality ministry. People in the parking lot directing, warmly greeting, and assisting people creates a great first impression. Consider using youth to help welcome people. A good demographic of workers speaks volumes. The parking ministry should help young or single mothers with carrying large bags, assisting with umbrellas in the rain, and making sure their needs are met. Think about how you would want someone to treat your mother. Additionally, having a security presence in the parking lot will help people feel at ease about their vehicles and know the church is concerned for their safety and protection.

Lastly, provide enough parking. If people cannot park, they will drive right through and find another church. The average church today has approximately two people per car. Therefore, plan for the number of people on campus at one time and provide the proper number of parking spaces. If parking adjacency is not possible or far from the facilities, provide transportation to the building, such as a golf cart ministry or bus ministry. On larger campuses, consider having bus stop shelters for comfort and inclement weather throughout the parking lot areas.

The adjacency of parking is also critical. The ideal parking layout has parking close to every building, on all sides of the campus. Try to balance the parking as best as possible given the site and existing building locations.

Finallly, landscaping is probably the most neglected aspect of building grounds. However, nice landscaping makes a great impression for visitors, and members will be proud of their church facility.

GREETING FIRST IMPRESSION

As stated previously, we are still in the critical first minutes on campus. Your church should have greeters at every entrance. Instruct greeters on how to act and what to look for. They should be friendly and smiling with an attitude of "Welcome! Great to see you. We are glad you are here." All demographics should be represented. Make greeters identifiable with name tags, vests for parking, or "ask me" badges or signs. The greeters should be actively welcoming people (both guests and members) and assisting with directions and information. They can assist the elderly getting in and out of vehicles, young mothers with carrying items, and umbrellas for inclement weather. Adequately sized entrances are critical to a quality experience.

The entrance to the building needs be welcoming, inviting, and attractive. If the first thing you see when you walk in is a small, crowded lobby with no directional signage or information center visible, it will discourage visitors. The lobby or foyer should be spacious, with seating groups and adequate room for people gathering together and moving through. This commons area has the potential to be one of the most important spaces for church health, as it will encourage relationship building. There can be a cafe, coffee, information, playground, digital signage, music playing, and so forth. People generally have three places: the home, work, and that third place. Many coffee shops like Starbucks have figured this out quite successfully. The church used to be the hub in the community, and it needs to be it again. This can become the community's third place.

Building signage is critical. If, for some reason, a greeter misses a visitor, it should be obvious where to go for worship, children, preschool/nursery, and bathrooms. Building signage should be easily visible anywhere on the campus and allow a person to know where to go quickly. With the upcoming iBeacon or location technology, the church can have digital signage available to smart phones, tablets, and even cars upon entering any part of the campus or building. This can transform sharing information on the ministry. For example, a car drives on campus and a message pops up that says, "We are glad you are here!" with directions to visitor, handicap, and young mother parking. You walk in the front doors and a message arrives with a directional map. You walk into the worship center and receive a sermon outline along with the purpose and vision of the church. You pick up your children, and a teaching series becomes available to inform you what your child learned that day and how to reinforce it at home.

Ushers and greeters should also be located at the worship-center entrances. The ushers need to ask people about their favorite subjects—themselves. They need to be friendly and escort visitors to seating. The usher should be familiar with members and introduce the visitors to others of similar age, background, career, or kids. Teach your congregation to look for visitors or people they don't yet know and introduce themselves. Make sure no visitors slip through the cracks.

It is also critical that ushers plan for and protect the worship service for late arrivals. Work with the tech team to lower lights once the service begins so that latecomers aren't as noticed or interruptive. Consider adding digital media with a countdown to the start of worship in the worship center and lobby areas.

The restrooms need to be adequate to support a large number of people in a short amount of time. They need to be clean and protected from bad sight lines to people outside the restroom. They need to include baby changing tables, mirrors, book shelves, and other comfort items.

CHILDREN'S MINISTRY FIRST IMPRESSION

The first impressions upon entering the nursery/preschool and children areas are critical. These spaces should look clean and safe. The parent should have confidence in the amount of security and staff taking care of children. There should be a secured entrance so no one can enter or leave the preschool and children area unobserved or unaccounted for.

Make the check-in process easy and seamless. Consider

adding online registration for children prior to arrival on your website to simplify and enhance the check-in process. There are numerous programs with check-in stations that take parents ten seconds or fewer to check-in their children. Most systems will print out stickers with a child's information, including who can pick up the child, medications, and other pertinent information. There should not be long waiting lines or a crowded drop-off area. Inadequate circulation space at the check-in check-out areas can create a poor experience. Create a designated line for visitors to make it an easy experience. New parents should be introduced to the space and the people working with their children.

The children are going to share everything that happened during their time in the preschool or children's areas. These ministries need to be excellent. Millennials today will go to church where their kids feel comfortable and want to go. It is important that the children have a positive experience.

Consider taking every opportunity to explain the care you take to protect the children, such as check-in and check-out procedures, background investigation of workers, peanut-free facilities, etc. Consider having closed-circuit security cameras throughout the facility that are continuously recording. This will show parents that security is important. Lockdown, fire, tornado, and other emergency procedures should also be in place.

WELCOME FIRST IMPRESSION

The first impressions upon entering the worship center are also critical. Provide a worshipful atmosphere before the service by playing soft music. Encourage members to connect and socialize before service begins. Ensure good visibility of the platform from any seat in the worship center. There should be good sound and acoustics that match the style of worship.

The seating should be comfortable and ample. The amount of space between rows of seats is critical for people moving in and out of seating as well as comfort while sitting and standing. The style of seating and the style of worship will affect the seating distance, but a minimum of three feet is recommended.

The lighting should be adequate for the style of worship (good lighting to read and the ability to dim lighting if theatrical). Consider using your projection screens for announcements, mission statements, and the purpose of the church. Use this technology to scroll upcoming events and promote available ministries and programs.

Temperature is important. Can the HVAC system maintain proper temperature in the worship center when it fills with people quickly? Likewise, can it maintain the correct temperature on a cold day? Nothing is quite as memorable as how uncomfortable I was at a particular service because the worship center was hot and I needed to fan myself the entire time or so cold that I needed a blanket.

Make sure systems are maintained and routinely serviced properly. The mechanical system coming on or off with large squeals from a bad air handler belt or return air being too small with too much velocity will make it sound like a freight train in the room, probably precisely at a critical time of prayer or during the sermon.

The first impression of a pastor or leader welcoming the people to the church is also vital. Welcome visitors and make them feel special and at home. Done well, this will foster excitement and great expectations.

Consider asking visitors fill out a connection/visitor card. Emphasize its importance and explain why you are asking visitors to fill it out, or they will not. Play special music or a short video to give them time to fill it out. This again show your care.

Invite visitors to meet the pastor at a guest reception after service. There is no one better to ask a visitor to return than a caring pastor. Provide the visitors with a thank-you gift for visiting (first one to three visits).

One of the best first impressions made that I have personally seen is when a new visitor receives a personal thank-you card, text, or call from the lead pastor or small group leader. This personal touch, regardless of the size of the church, is incredibly important. I've seen this done every week by the senior pastor of a church of five thousand—so no church is too big to incorporate this practice.

WORSHIP FIRST IMPRESSION

The first impression of the praise and worship will verify or discourage a return visit. Guests are expecting a certain style of worship, or they would likely not be visiting. No matter your worship style, whether traditional or contemporary, do it with excellence. Nothing prepares a person to receive the Word of God quite like an authentic praise and worship experience.

The praise team and/or choir set the stage for worship. Remind them to smile and be authentic. Their attitudes are contagious.

A quality worship experience begins with a building that is designed and tuned properly for the style of worship. A poor acoustical experience will leave a visitor uneasy. The audio, video, and lighting is one of the most difficult aspects of worship to perfect.

Once again, the HVAC system should be designed to not interfere with the room acoustics. Quality audio, video, and lighting systems can add clarity and gain emotional attention to focus our hearts on worshiping God. Too often the budgets of church projects cut the audio, video, and lighting first. This is a big mistake. It must be thoroughly designed into the building from the beginning and maintained for the style of worship through the design and construction of the facility to provide the best atmosphere for worship. Acoustics are critical for a great worship experience. They are worth the expense.

PREACHING FIRST IMPRESSION

A quality sermon is an important first impression to a visitor and a growth opportunity for members. Sermon preparation, preaching, and teaching led by the Holy Spirit will present God's Word in a way that will not return void. A powerful sermon can overcome other bad first impressions, but not easily. Conversely, a bad sermon will stand out over other good first impressions and hurt the prospect of a visitor returning. Distractions, such as not being able to clearly hear the words spoken or being uncomfortable due to the temperature or seat cushion, can make the difference.

Believers need to be well-versed on how to be saved and how to have full assurance of salvation based on God's Word. But salvation is only the beginning. My observation is that a healthy church is not only sharing Jesus as our Savior but is also teaching the reality that we must make Him Jesus our Lord (Romans 10:9–10). It is but the first step of a life-long process of growing to be more like Christ (2 Peter 3:18; 2 Corinthians 3:18). The pastor's job is to give the church the best possible training from the Word so that they might be able to minister effectively and represent Christ rightly in the world, bringing others to the Savior.

Consider live streaming the audio and/or video of the service in relational areas, corridors, preschool and children areas, youth spaces, and cry rooms. Use the technology to advertise for visitors or to post the number for a parent to assist with an unhappy child. Consider using an outline on IMEG (the projection screen) and a bulletin insert. Encourage the church to follow you in their Bibles (or on their smartphones), as we see the Bereans doing in Acts 17:11.

Finally, it is critical that the audio is clear and the volume is appropriate. Poor acoustics will distract a person and turn a great message into a bad experience with nothing learned.

TITHING FIRST IMPRESSION

Some ministry leaders need to own the process of taking tithes and offerings in a service. Hours are spent preparing for worship, sermons, and small-group lessons. How much thought and time is put into the time of giving during the service? This is the lifeline of church ministry and a vital time for each person to obey God and bless Him through their obedience and stewardship. Stewardship is part of the worship experience for all individuals.

First, consider using different approaches each week for the "giving talk" and spend time preparing to reach people regarding "why" they give. This is an intentional, planned moment to explain giving in your church service. This talk can be given by the pastor, a staff member, or a volunteer with a testimony. This act of worship is critical to spiritual development and must be taken seriously.

The giving talk must give clear direction. Consider explaining the process before you take up the tithe to set visitors at ease. For example: "In the coming moments you are going to see us pass an offering plate down the aisles, and you will have the opportunity to support the ministry and purpose of this church." Don't forget to mention the opportunities to give online or via text or smartphone apps, if your church has those available. Multimedia messages outlining the various ways to give is an excellent way to educate the church.

Second, provide the reason for giving. People give for several reasons: we are commanded by Scripture, we desire God's blessing in our lives, we understand the impact it makes, we are interested in the statistics about where the dollars go, and we appreciate the stories or testimonies of how God has worked in our own lives or in the lives of others.

Third, there needs to be a call to take action. This is when you tell people exactly what you are asking them to do. It's a clear and specific step. "As this plate passes down the aisle, if you are a guest, we ask that you drop your connection card in it. If you would like to give to our ministry, use the envelope provided and place your donation in the plate."

CLOSING FIRST IMPRESSION

The closing is an opportunity for several things:

- the unsaved to make a commitment to Christ and take action;
- the newly saved to take the next step in their growth in your church's plan for discipleship;

- your slightly committed member or newly churched person to move into a serving ministry;
- the hurting to ask for healing and find a person to pray for them, direct them, and get the God to begin the healing process;
- the guest to join with this church family.

Plan for the closing. Have people in place at the altars to pray for and with people. Encourage people to move to the next level of commitment in their walks with Christ. Providing counseling rooms for those who made a commitment to Christ is a nice touch. Ask people to return next week or to attend a Bible study or small group. Remind visitors to meet the pastor at the guest reception area.

Announcements work best at the beginning of the service. I have found that delivering them at the end of the service is not as effective since most people typically have already checked out as the service closes.

NATURAL SYNERGY

Consider ways to make visitors feel comfortable and special. If you get them to come three times to your church, you have a significant chance of keeping them if they then develop two to three relationships. Then your focus should be on movement to grow in small groups, discipleship opportunities, and service.

Remember, you cannot be everything to everyone. God has uniquely equipped you to reach the community. Whatever you do, do it with excellence. If not, don't do it.

The natural synergy between your building and evangelism is important. Various first impressions to visitors and potential future church family members are vital. Remember, this synergy is not only for the visitors. Church members will take pride in the facilities and will be encouraged to invite their friends and acquaintances to visit. Being invited to church is still the number one reason a person visits a church. If we neglect our buildings, we are presenting a closed-door image. It appears that we are not expecting company, we only care about ourselves, or we don't care about our ministry.

This concept may seem materialistic, but it's not. If ministry is defined by designing and constructing our building around our ministry, then our building defines us. It is difficult to reach young families and children if you do not provide a clean, safe, secure, and quality environment. We need to offer facilities as good or better than the world offers. May our buildings never be a hindrance to reaching people but a tool to introduce them to Jesus Christ and help them grow in their faith. May the gospel of Jesus Christ be the first offense, not our buildings.

Please also remember that social media, including your website, apps, Facebook, and Twitter, are absolutely critical first impressions with increasing importance. There is much to discuss regarding quality websites and social media. Make sure you do your research and utilize this incredible tool correctly. This is quickly becoming your new front door.

4 THE SYNERGY OF A BUILDING AND FELLOWSHIP

How can our facility help us connect with others and share our lives together? There is a synergy of a building and fellowship that will help us to grow warmer.

When you mention church health and fellowship, many immediately turn to the breaking of bread and a fellowship hall. However, quality, warm fellowship is so much more.

Fellowship by definition is companionship, partnership, and sharing. Fellowship is connecting people together through Christ to learn how to love and serve each other.

A pastor for one church we built in Fort Walton Beach, Florida, pointed out that their people never saw one another. They had two worship services, with a maze of hallways to connect to the classrooms. There were three small lobby entrances from three different sides of the complex. Many people would find their way to their classes, find another way to the worship center, then to their cars. There were also many elevation changes throughout the various buildings. Our project included building new preschool rooms, renovating a classroom, the fellowship hall, offices, the worship center, and adding a large commons area in the middle of the campus. We had to demolish many winding corridors and fix elevation changes, but it brought the entire campus together. The church now has seating areas for relational spaces, a clear entry point, and a cafe. When people come into the campus, the worship center is to the right and the classrooms, preschool area, and fellowship hall is to the left. People are able to connect once again! They feel like one church again. The leadership mentioned that their biggest problem now is that they can't get people to leave the church after services are over. What a nice problem to have.

Many studies show that people stay in a church because they build a relationship with two to three other people. It's part of the glue that keeps them plugged in when life gets tough. Fellowship and connecting go hand-in-hand with small group discipleship, which we cover in the next chapter.

Years ago, people thought each church needed an entry point where people could be greeted as they entered the worship center. This narthex has moved into a much larger capacity in recent years. Today's church culture is looking for a place to connect. It's important to all generations, but especially the millennial generation. I call this place the commons or connect space. The size of this space is quickly moving to be equal to the size of the worship center.

This goes along with the third place theory we discussed above. There is the home, work, and then a third place. As we become more and more technology driven, our relationships and the opportunities to connect with others become increasingly important. The church should be that "third place" where people can come, be accepted, and connect to other believers.

Some may believe this is wasted space. However, I have seen this space serve multiple ministries and provide countless opportunities. A commons can be enhanced as a tool by having seating group areas, where people can sit down and have conversations. Technology, such as digital signage and Wi-Fi, needs to be available, as well as a coffee cafe. It can also include a bookstore or media center to access material to grow in faith (books, CDs, Bibles, study guides, etc.). Another great addition is having an indoor playground where parents can connect while their children are playing in a safe, clean environment. This commons area can be designed to be adaptable for other uses, such as simulcasting worship services, fellowship dinners, wedding receptions, or community events. I have seen many community teams and organizations use the church commons for such special events and meetings.

Having quality restroom facilities directly off the commons is important. Men, I highly recommend that you invest into a quality ladies' restroom. Talk with a team of ladies in your church to find out what they need in the restroom facility. These things may include the proper mirrors, bookshelves, baby changing stations, lighting, etc.

Small groups, life groups, Bible study groups, and Sunday school classes all can use the commons to share, fellowship, and study the Word.

Business centers and conference rooms are also things to consider off the commons area. This will allow the community and church members to connect and use this hub.

Fellowship space can also be a fellowship hall. Providing an area where the church can feed masses of people further enhances the ministry. This would include the proper fellowship space, kitchen, food pantry, storage, and restroom facilities.

Many churches have benefited their members by providing a meal once a week. Given the busyness of life, this gives them a cost-effective meal they don't have to prepare. This is another opportunity to build relationships and allow your congregation to connect to one another. I've seen this fellowship space grow a church by feeding the community,

THE SYNERGY OF A BUILDING AND FELLOWSHIP / **79**

hosting dinners for community events, and feeding its membership for special events or a weekly dinner.

The natural synergy between your building and fellowship is important to growing a healthy ministry. If you do not provide this space, you are missing another opportunity for your members to build relationships with one another. This provides a tool to learn how to connect, to love one another, and to reach the community. God is clear through many Scriptures in His Word that He blesses unity (e.g., Psalm 133). This tool will encourage that unity.

5 THE SYNERGY OF A BUILDING AND DISCIPLESHIP

How can our facility help us grow in our discipleship training? There is a synergy of a building and discipleship that will help us to grow deeper.

Discipleship is growing in your personal relationship with Christ, which is also called sanctification. It is a lifelong pursuit of following Christ and involves learning the Bible, good theology, and how to apply God's Word to your life.

Whether you value having small group Bible study on campus, connecting in life groups in homes, or don't currently emphasize this aspect of church life, having discipleship space at your church campus can be an excellent tool to grow healthier. It is obvious with the Sunday school model that lack of space can create a problem. In order to minister holistically to the community and to help people spiritually mature, training space is vital. Having training rooms available with multimedia capabilities allows you to teach financial training, divorce recovery, drug rehabilitation, Bible studies, health classes, education classes, and language classes. The sky is the limit to equip and empower people in your training classrooms.

Children's ministry is discipleship, not merely babysitting. A church must have rooms to provide quality teaching to the preschool and children. This is key to training up children and attracting and keeping young families in your church.

I have worked with a church in Nashville, Tennessee, that had an incredible worship center and good preschool, children, and youth space, but it was completely out of space to teach the Word in a small-group setting. In fact, it had a culture of not providing Bible study on campus on Sundays. They provided some classes throughout the week, but biblical maturity was not occurring at the level desired. However, they were led to develop more classroom space in order to equip and empower their congregation. Providing this proper space facilitated Christian education and spiritual maturity. This spiritual growth led to more sharing of the gospel and thus more growth in worship. As a matter of fact, it took hold so nicely that they desired to build even more classroom space for additional training areas.

Another church in Ft. Mill, South Carolina, was out of

education space and trying to sustain growth with two Bible study hours. Classes were large, overcrowded, and there was no room for new classes. After adding new education space, the participation of Bible study increased from 50 percent of worship attendance to over 80 percent. Was it worth it? To that 30 percent it was.

Disciple making doesn't happen just because a church exists and people attend. It is a deliberate process. It involves equipping the saints, which in turn will move them into evangelism and service. It is centered around the Word and is a people-to-people ministry. It is the Word of God shaping men and women within life-on-life relationships, teaching one another to obey what Jesus commanded. It is a call for each person to live like Christ.

Discipleship doesn't happen only in coffee shops and living rooms. It also happens in the sanctuary where the Word is sung, prayed, read, preached, and acted upon through communion and baptism.

The first order of spiritual business is discipleship. This process involves building effective disciples of Jesus Christ from the members God has already placed in the congregation. Effective disciples become effective disciplers. Then, a congregation of effective disciplers is ready to receive and assimilate new converts.

Alan Taylor pointed out this leadership principle at a

men's conference at First Baptist Church Woodstock. Each leader in your church has different gifts and levels of gifting. If you are going to grow a church, you need to increase your leadership base. One person can attract and disciple a certain number of people, where another person can attract and disciple others. The total number of people is determined by the width of the leadership base.[12]

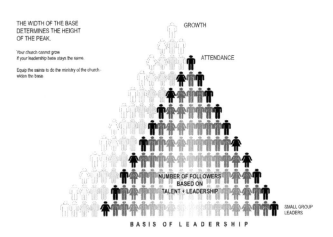

Scripture commands that we have a solid doctrinal foundation "until we all attain to the unity of the faith, and the knowledge of the Son of God, to a mature man, to the measure of the stature which belongs to the fullness of Christ. As a result, we are no longer to be children, tossed here and there by waves and carried about by every wind of doctrine, by the trickery of men, by craftiness, in deceitful scheming, but speaking the truth in love, we are to grow up in all aspects into Him who is the head, even Christ" (Ephesians 4:13–15 NASB).

Second Timothy 4:2 challenges us to "preach the word; be ready in season *and* out of season; reprove, rebuke, exhort, with great patience and instruction" (NASB).

A quality facility will make the movement from worship to small groups easy and desirable. The location of the discipleship spaces is critical. Ideally, space for senior adults and young families will be near the worship center. The adjacency to the worship center, with proper accessibility, is key for these two demographics.

Although many ministries meet in homes or places other than the church, on-site small group discipleship is a must for preschool, children, and youth. To understand how a building can facilitate discipling children and youth, we must first understand that this ministry is not babysitting. It is called children's "ministry" and youth "ministry," not babysitting. The Bible clearly put the responsibility on parents to train up their children in the Word. Never does Scripture mandate the church as the responsible party to teach children about the Lord. However, a good facility will enhance the ability for churches to encourage, train, and equip the children and youth, as well as prepare and train the parents "how to" teach their children.

As previously mentioned, the preschool and children facility should be located close to the worship center and commons. Ideally, people should enter into the commons and go one direction for children and preschool and another to worship.

Also, we must understand that the millennial generation, as well as all parents, are trending toward attending a church their children want to attend. Many parents will attend a church based on where their children are getting the best programs, even if they don't agree with all the church's doctrine. Safety, security, and cleanliness are extremely important to parents. Parents have a hard time enjoying worship if they do not feel confident that their children are taken care of completely.

The goal for the preschool space is to allow parents to feel that their children are safe, well-cared for, and enjoying their time when they leave them in your facility. Therefore, the preschool must have a control point (check-in desk) where no person enters or leaves without knowledge or permission. A drop-off area—out of the main traffic pattern to prevent congestion—is important to the parental experience. Check-in stations with a software program that allows parents to quickly check-in their children and include information such as medications, allergies, special needs, and names of people allowed to pick up the children is critical.

The first time parents check in their children, the workers should explain the measures they take to protect all the children. This should include background checks on workers, security controls, lockdown procedures, and the ability to contact the parent if needed quickly (e.g., a pager system). It is a good idea to introduce the parents to the person working with their child, at least the first time. They should have the opportunity to observe the nice environment and care given to the children.

A quality preschool room will allow for workers to provide a comfortable, home-like environment with dimmed lighting control, distributed music, and quality cribs, changing tables, and furniture. The ability for the preschool worker to keep toys clean and safe and food and drinks cold, as well as have a proper area for diaper changing and a sink for cleaning, is a must. Child safety locks on cabinets and drawers are necessary, as are tamper-resistant outlet covers. The room should have storage space, including cubbies to store each child's personal items. The flooring should be sanitary and bacteria resistant. The room should include a minimum of closed-circuit security cameras, monitored and recorded. A nice addition is a TV with DVD player to use for teaching and entertaining children. Whenever controllable, natural light can be added to the room.

One often-asked question is: "How many preschoolers

should you place in each room?" The successful ministries we have worked with agree that, regardless of the room size, twelve is the maximum. There should be at least one adult for every six preschoolers. If the room is oversized or undersized, you are losing efficiency. You should plan on approximately thirty-five square feet of space per child.

To further provide a quality environment, the preschool space would ideally include a laundry room, kitchenette, office space, and restrooms for the adult workers. It's a good idea to have a bathroom attached to each room for children two years-old and older. This will allow workers to help the children use the bathroom without leaving the security of the room.

If you desire parents deliver their preschoolers to the room themselves, you should have a drop-off counter at each room or a Dutch door. This will allow for easy transfer of the children without allowing other children to leave the room.

A children's facility has the same safety and security concerns as the preschool area. As you move into the elementary age, you can be effective with rooms that have no more than eighteen children in one room. There should be one adult for each nine children. You should plan on approximately twenty-five square feet of space per child. Boys' and girls' restrooms should be included in the children's area. This will keep children from leaving the secured area to use the bathroom.

An assembly space or children's church is an effective way to teach our children how to worship God. I recommend leaving this space adaptable so it can be used for other activities, such as AWANA, Vacation Bible School, Bible quiz matches, etc. Today's technology allows for multi-server technology and environmental projection. This enables you to quickly and effectively change the environment by projecting a digital image on three walls in a room to match whatever subject you are teaching. This space should have quality audio, video, and lighting.

The children rooms should have the ability to keep toys clean and safe and a hand-washing sink that may include an integrated drinking fountain fixture (bubbler). Child safety locks on cabinets and drawers are still a good idea. Tack board strips are also desirable. The room should have age-appropriate furniture and the flooring should be sanitary and bacteria resistant. The room should include a minimum of closed circuit security cameras that are monitored and recorded. A TV with a DVD player is a nice addition to use for teaching children. It is beneficial to have natural light whenever possible. Tamper-resistant outlet covers is another good choice. A resource room for storing supplies, in addition to storage in each room, is helpful.

More frequently our team is creating space for children with special needs, which is an incredible ministry opportunity.

Occasionally, a ministry will desire to have an isolation room, or cool down space, for children with special needs.

A children's worship experience is becoming increasingly popular, teaching our children how to love God in worship. Much of the technology described in the worship center section applied here also.

Youth classrooms are usually the most neglected. These rooms have the same needs as the adult rooms. They should provide for various sizes and include marker boards and tack boards. Ideally, the room should have audio and video capability for teaching. Comfortable seating and lighting is also important. You should plan on approximately twenty-five square feet of space per youth in assembly-style seating, or fifteen square feet of space per youth in table-style seating. This is usually supplemented with a high-tech worship environment, as well as hang-out space with games and furniture to sit and connect.

Adult classrooms should provide for various size classes. The rooms should include a minimum of some type of marker board and tack board. Even more effective is audio and video capability for teaching. Internet access should be available for each educational space because Wi-Fi provides many options and tools become for the teaching and learning environment.

Comfortable seating and lighting is important in this

environment. It's been said that one's mind can only take in what one's seat can endure. You should plan on approximately seven square feet of space per adult in assembly-style seating or twenty square feet of space per adult in table-style seating.

Some adult and children classrooms enjoy using tables. The table height and material should suit the age group. For example, do not place large, tall, heavy, wooden tables with sharp corners in a children's classroom.

If the classroom does not provide for it, segmented areas of classes should include a coffee and refreshment area. Restrooms should be clean and readily accessible.

Accessibility to all classroom spaces is essential. Each and every space should be accessible for handicap and special needs.

Temperature should be adequately zoned by exterior exposure and use of space. It's not wise to attempt to satisfy a preschool room of twelve children on the same zone with a senior adult classroom of fifty adults.

A balance of resources should provide for a healthy ratio of adult, youth, and children discipleship spaces. Tony Morgan presented statistics from his research in his book *Vital Signs* that I have experienced in the healthy churches with which I have partnered. Morgan explains that a healthy church demographically will have between 20 to 30 percent children to adults ratio of attendance. Youth will fall between 10 to 15 percent. Further, healthy churches have more than 50 percent of adults in small group Bible study. Don't forget to track the metric of those serving in ministry. Healthy churches have this percentage at more than 50 percent as well. The strongest churches I have worked with have more than 30 percent children and more than 90 percent assimilation of small groups and serving.[13]

The goal in discipleship spaces is to do as Paul said in Titus 2:10: "make the teaching about God our Savior attractive in every way" (NLT). This way, "the opponent will be put to shame, having nothing bad to say about us" (v. 8 NASB). Romans 12:1–2 says, "Therefore, I urge you, brethren, by the mercies of God to present your bodies as a living and holy sacrifice, acceptable to God, which is your spiritual service of worship. And do not be conformed to this world, but be transformed by the renewing of your mind, so that you may prove what the will of God is, that which is good and acceptable, and perfect" (NASB). The renewing of our mind and our transformation is encouraged and begins in these small group settings. This correlation of the natural synergy between your building and discipleship is critical to growing spiritually mature believers. Providing the correct discipleship tool will grow your church stronger and larger. A strong discipleship process will develop disciple makers, thus growing a stronger, healthier church rooted in a strong biblical foundation. Psalm 1:1–3 says, "How blessed is the man who does not walk in the counsel of the wicked, nor stand in the path of sinners, nor sit in the seat of scoffers! But his delight is in the law of the Lord, and in His law he meditates day and night. He will be like a tree firmly planted by streams of water, which yields its fruit in its season, and its leaf does not wither; and in whatever he does, he prospers" (NASB).

6 THE SYNERGY OF A BUILDING AND WORSHIP

How can our facility help us worship God? There is a synergy of a building and worship that will help us to grow stronger.

Worship is an expression of reverence, love, and adoration to a Holy God. It is giving Christ the best that He has given you; it involves singing praise and worship songs, giving tithes and offerings, and fellowshipping in spirit with other believers.

Hiland Park Baptist Church in Panama City, Florida, was one ministry we had the privilege to work with for three phases to develop a new worship center, commons area, fellowship hall, education space, and preschool and children space. In the past few years the church went through growth cycles from about six hundred to nine hundred, and then would fall back to six hundred in Sunday morning attendance. They were having multiple worship services on Sunday, but there was no circulation or common space. Changing from one service to another was a scene of a crowded, hot hallway, with not-so-happy people waiting for the previous service to conclude. After providing the proper worship venue that seated sixteen hundred people, along with the proper additional education space and commons areas, the church sustained incredible growth. After only the first two years in the building, they have grown to consistently around two thousand people on Sunday morning—and they are still growing! The church now has the seating capacity, complemented by the commons space and audio, video, and lighting technology, to support an incredible worship experience. The church has further been able to provide a new venue for hosting events such as singing groups, comedians, and speakers. The church may also add more preschool and children space to accommodate the growth.

Ephesians 5:18–21 says, "Be filled with the Spirit, speaking to one another in psalms and hymns and spiritual songs, singing and making melody with your heart to the Lord; always giving thanks for all things in the name of our Lord Jesus Christ to God, even the Father; and be subject to one another in the fear of Christ" (NASB). As this verse suggests, our environment, including the church facility, has a lot to do with what happens in a worship service. When you walk into some buildings, your mood will instantly lighten. Other buildings will move you toward depression. The shape, colors, finishes, lighting, and temperature of a room can instantly change your mood. When we know that we want to create an environment of worship, we can shape our buildings to be conducive to that.

There is nothing better to prepare our hearts to receive God's message than a quality praise and worship service. It gets our minds off worldly issues and problems and opens us to the Holy Spirit's leading, giving us the desire to know Him more.

Lighting has a large effect on mood. Incorrectly placed architectural lighting will cause the singers and speakers to have dark eyes. Shadows across a speaker's face reduces the impact of the message. You must be able to control the lighting to create the desired environment for each part of the worship service.

Great audio (amplified acoustics), visual, and theatrical lighting is one of the most important investments a church can make. Spend the money to have a quality sound system. A great worship experience prepares the heart to hear the message. It doesn't matter how good the message is if people cannot hear it in a pleasing manner. Nothing can destroy movement in someone's heart faster than a loud blast of feedback. Therefore, it is also important to have qualified people to run the equipment. There are numerous advancements today, such as presets on digital consoles for different parts of the service, that will make this critical ministry both simpler and more consistent.

Video technology is essential to incorporate into the worship service. People learn more from seeing than hearing. The words on the screen need to be clear and large enough to read from any seat in the worship center. There are many options, including LED walls, multi-server technology, and environmental projection, that allow churches to provide an incredible visual experience. Most of us are accustomed to video stimulation today with smartphones, iPads, and LED TVs. Holographic imagery is coming but still too expensive for most churches. We cannot provide a poor-quality video production and not expect a person in worship to wonder why we don't care enough to provide the best. We are not to be *of* this world but *in* this world as salt and light. Like it or not, we are being compared to what the world offers. We can provide as good a quality as the world offers. Our God deserves our best.

Technology provides several other tools for the worship experience. Smartphone apps, such as YouVersion, provide the pastor with a tool to provide members with sermon outlines and notes. Other technologies, such as Evites, online giving, and barcode scans, allow transfer of information for calendaring, evangelism, and discipleship.

Seating must match the style of worship. It needs to be comfortable and as close to the platform as possible. A connection point is lost for seating beyond ninety feet, so the majority of seating should be kept within seventy-five feet of the platform. I advise using theatre seating for fixed seating and pew chairs for non-fixed seating. Personal space is highly valued in our society. People expect to have their own seats or individual chairs. You should plan on twenty-one to twenty-four-inch chairs. Of course, provide handicap accessibility areas, as well as some armrests that are movable so larger people can use two seats.

For determining seating capacity, the 80 percent rule is too basic for determining if you have room for sustainable growth. For pews, the sustainable attendance is 70 to 75 percent of the seating capacity at twenty-one inches. If using pew chairs (or stackable, non-fixed seating), the sustainable attendance is 80 to 85 percent of the number of seats at twenty-one inches. When using theatre seats, the sustainable attendance is 90 to 95 percent of the number of seats. Seating sizes will normally range from twenty-one to twenty-four inches to allow for the aisles to align properly.

The back-to-back distance standard for seating is three feet. When the envelope of the seat is reduced (e.g., with a theatre seat folding up versus a stationary pew), this will allow for easy movement of people from seat to seat. The style of worship affects the distance from row to row. A more charismatic style will work better with thirty-eight to forty-two inches between rows. As you move up to a gallery, balcony, or stadium-setting configuration, the back-to-back should increase to at least three-feet-by-two-inches to three-feet-by-six-inches to provide for better movement. Choir or praise team risers should be spaced at three-feet-by-six-inches to four feet back-to-back to allow for adequate space to stand in front of the chair, depending on the type of chair used.

If you use moveable, non-fixed seating, set them up in a radius so people can see some of each other's faces. Always set up less chairs than you need with the ability to bring out more. It's encouraging to add chairs, but depressing to have many empty seats.

A good worship experience will not place a person in a row of seats with less than four people. If you provide seating rows for two or three, they will most likely go unused. At the same time, it's a good rule of thumb not to expect a person to have to move past more than twelve people to get out of a seat into an aisle.

A worship center must provide good lines of site from every seat. Placing seating behind a column or not having the platform high enough to see the pastor, worship team, choir, or instrumentalist provides a poor and frustrating worship experience. The addition of IMAG (Image Magnification) projection and LED wall have helped in this area, but it is always best to have appropriate lines of sight to parts of the platform.

A good worship experience will include proper temperature control. Simply put, the system needs to be capable of taking an empty room, filling it will people in fifteen minutes or less, and maintaining temperature at a comfortable level (typically around seventy-one to seventy-two degrees). The temperature can destroy the best planned service in a matter of minutes. When people are too hot or too cold, they stop participating in the service by mentally checking out and looking forward to it being over. The most common mistake is to keep a space too warm. Keeping the temperature on the cool side will keep the people alert and awake.

Clean restrooms are an important part of your facility and a guest's experience. Guests may forget your sermon, but the memories of foul-smelling restrooms stick. You can tell a lot about the morale of a church by looking at the quality of the restrooms. One of the first stops by all visitors, and most members, is the restroom. A good experience will provide age-appropriate restrooms adequately distributed throughout the campus.

The natural synergy between your building and worship is easily identifiable. The wrong building can hinder a quality worship experience because people will be more concerned about their comfort rather than receiving God's Word. The correct building will provide an environment that sets hearts and minds on Christ, ready to receive the Lord.

7 THE SYNERGY OF A BUILDING AND MINISTRY

How can our facility help us grow in our ministry? There is a synergy of a building and ministry that will help us to grow broader.

Ministry is an activity carried out by Christians to express and grow our faith in Jesus Christ. It is meeting the needs of people and involves serving, loving, and giving to others.

My pastor, Patrick Pfrimmer, has taught me a simple principle in life by defining love: "Love is meeting needs." We can quickly learn how to grow our ministries if we meet others' needs as Christ met all of humanity's needs by first loving us and then willingly going to the cross. We must learn to meet others' needs by loving and serving them completely as well.

Stevens Street Baptist Church in Cookeville, Tennessee, has an incredible college ministry. The church has reached out to college students from Tennessee Tech to include them in their church for both worship and ministry. It is not uncommon to see over two-hundred and fifty college students attend worship on any given Sunday morning. You will also find them participating in serving in the church's ministries—whether it is greeting or serving in the preschool. The church provides a free lunch to the college students every Sunday after church. What an example of meeting the needs of these college students.

Churches have buildings that allow us to minister to members as well as the community. To stay outward focused and serve local communities, church facilities must be accessible to their neighbors. Rules and guidelines to use facilities are necessary and must be appropriately followed, but buildings should be places for reaching, loving, and serving the community.

Gymnasiums and ball fields provide opportunities for youth programs to have a place to play in safe and godly environments. Exercise facilities, including walking tracks and aerobic rooms, allow for members and the community to work on physical fitness. Fellowship halls and kitchens allow a church to feed the community and provide meals to homebound people. Worship centers provide places for weddings and funerals. The unchurched may desire to have a wedding or funeral in a church setting versus a community building but does not have an affiliation with a specific church. This is a great opportunity for outreach and loving them.

Upward Sports has been a successful way to minister to and reach youth. Kids and their parents find a safe, clean environment, as well as a church that loves them. Parents will go where their kids are safe, secure, being fed spiritually, and wanting to go.

Other uses for church facilities include food pantries to feed the poor and needy. Clothing ministries help clothe the needy. Daycare and preschool programs provide safe and clean Christian environments for the children of working parents. Our buildings can also provide areas for the elderly to have lunches together, fellowship, women and men Bible studies, recovery centers, teaching centers for financial matter, and so forth.

We are finding more churches today attempting to holistically meet the needs of the community. Many churches have provided spaces that allow them to provide medical and psychological treatment. Classroom environments allow for education classes, English as a second language training, addiction care groups, and the ability to meet with counselors in areas of nutrition, marriage relationships, parenting, and other relationship issues.

More and more, both parents are working full-time jobs, and families are in need of daycare for their children as well as after-school programs. Therefore, preschool and child daycare programs, when done properly, are a large impact in the local community. Many times, these programs provide jobs to the community, a well-needed service, as well as an introduction to the church for assimilation into the church family. These programs can also provide a source of revenue to fund other ministries.

As the American senior adult population continues to grow, adult daycares and independent and assisted living facilities are becoming increasingly effective for church ministries. These programs allow for a quality, dignified environment for seniors and provide jobs for the community and income to support other church ministries.

The natural synergy between your building and ministry is evident by having the necessary tools to be able to meet the needs of your community. Certainly the church needs to be out in the community to serve. However, the proper building will provide a safe harbor to minister to hurting people.

8   THE SYNERGY OF A BUILDING AND PRAYER

How can our facility help us grow in our prayer life? There is a synergy of a building and prayer that will help us to grow closer.

Prayer is growing in your personal relationship with Christ. Prayer is communicating with our Lord, which involves both listening and talking.

Bethel World Outreach Church in Brentwood, Tennessee, is an excellent ministry in many ways. I was intrigued by how they dismiss their children for children's worship from the worship center. After the children left with the children ministry leaders, the pastor led the congregation in a prayer for the children, interceding that the Holy Spirit would speak into their young hearts and minds and that the church would love them in a godly way, teaching them how to worship God, love Him, and learn His Word. It was simple yet powerful. As a parent, it was very moving. It demonstrated that this church cared about their children. It was more than babysitting to them; it was ministry with excellence.

A healthy church will always be a praying church. Prayer is a critical part of seeking God's face to reach the lost, serve the community, and ask for God to work in the church and in its members' lives. Prayer services are not merely a series of prayer requests followed by a corporate prayer. It's not accomplished by praying together over a meal. Prayer is described in Acts 2:42: "They devoted themselves to the apostles' teaching, to the fellowship, to the breaking of bread, and to prayers" (HCSB). The word *devoted* means "with intensity and deliberation." When the early church devoted themselves to prayer, they were fervent, intense, passionate, and deliberate about praying. Prayer is a huge part of any healthy church.

Jesus gave us an example of how to pray in Matthew 6:5–15 and Luke 11:1–4. As Luther said, "He is hollowed when both our doctrine and our life are Christian."[14] When it comes to our facilities, our churches should have the attitude and prayer of "Whatever it is that brings the fullness of your redemptive purpose to pass, do that Lord!" It's not about us; it is about God's will being done.

A church that incorporates ministries such as a prayer tower or twenty-four-hour access to a prayer chapel encourages its members to be praying for their pastor, the ministry, and the community. These prayer areas are used by many churches for several reasons, including having deacons meet to pray for the pastor during the worship services and allowing members to rotate throughout the day to pray for their leadership, ministries, and community. Many churches I have worked with have counseling areas where people who make decisions in their lives or need healing or help can pray with someone and receive counsel, outside of praying at the altar.

Churches will grow closer to Christ through a healthy prayer life, both corporately and individually. In a worship center, having the proper amount of comfortable space at the altar will allow for people to approach the altar to pray for healing, wholeness, and one another's needs. If space isn't provided for ministry to occur at the altar, it can't be expected for people to use it.

Something unfortunate that can interrupt and possibly ruin a moment of prayer in a worship center is the HVAC coming on and sounding like a freight train. The distraction causes minds to wander and allows the spiritual atmosphere to dissipate. Poor temperature control, seating or acoustics can also distract people who are wanting to—and needing to—connect with God. Disturbance from the commons, lobby, or door entrances can also hinder prayer. A sound lock, quiet door closures, and ushers protecting the entrances of the worship center is extremely helpful for the continuity of the prayerful atmosphere.

The natural synergy between your building and prayer is evident by having the tools to cultivate and encourage prayer. Certainly a culture of prayer is ignited with the examples of the pastoral staff. However, the wrong tools coupled with distractions or lack of provision can hinder prayer.

9 THE SYNERGY OF A BUILDING AND OUTWARD FOCUS TO GROW HEALTHIER

How can our facility help us to stay outward focused? There is a synergy of a building and outward focus that will help us to grow healthier.

Outward focus is being concerned with those who do not know Christ. It is staying focused on and being determined to carry out the Great Commission. It involves programs, buildings, budgets, and vision.

There are some obvious advantages that the proper buildings can provide when it comes to providing ministries to the community. With the appropriate gymnasiums and fellowship halls, churches can provide Upward Sports programs, AWANA programs, and facilities for community events, such as banquets, dinners, meals for the homeless and homebound, and all forms of recreation.

However, outward focus involves more than the simple thought process. Today, our churches compete with so many other opportunities that the world offers. Yes, I think the church should offer as good as the world offers. However, what separates the church from the world is the love of Jesus Christ in us. Genuine compassion is incredibly influential. Think about the people in your life who have had the most positive influence on you . . . they probably have been those who loved you completely, unconditionally, and with no strings attached.

I am absolutely convinced that one of the best ways to reach people in the community is to let them experience His love through us. John 13:24–45 says, "I give you a new command: Love each other *deeply* and *fully*. Remember the ways that I have loved you, and demonstrate your love for others in those same ways" (VOICE; emphasis added).

As you become the person God intends you to become, you will reach the people God intends for you to reach. In the same light, as your church develops the right tools, your campus will have many outreach venues (kitchen, food pantry, clothing ministry, storage, youth and children ministries, restoration ministries, teaching and tutoring space, after-school assistance, daycare, etc.). We can sow seeds of kindness wherever we are in everyday life. We can also provide ministries at our churches to care for, love, help, provide for, and minister to our community. True love is meeting the needs of others. Instead of only focusing on our own needs, we will find incredible satisfaction and eternal reward by meeting others' needs.

Friendship Community Church is one of the most outwardly focused churches I have worked with. They go into the community and wear T-shirts that say, "The church has left the building." They hold car washes for one dollar, but instead of charging one dollar, they will wash a car, pay the driver a dollar for the opportunity to wash their car, and tell them God loves them and they are special to Him. That is servant evangelism! Furthermore, each small group in the church takes on an outreach community ministry project every ten weeks. They are making an impact. They feed, educate, love, serve, and share Christ in the community.

Begin thinking outside the box about how your facility can be used to reach the community. Assess what needs your community has that are not being met or met well. Then, through prayer and God's leading, determine how you can use your facility to meet those needs.

Many times, an inward focus prevents us from seeing the needs outside of ourselves or our immediate surroundings. We are so used to our own facilities that we continue to accept the deficiencies, hoping we won't have a problem. Or we delay the expense of fixing problems due to finances, desires, or know-how. Then little problems become big problems.

Many times, there are liabilities associated with a church not updating facilities. Building codes have been mandated for safety reasons, and they are often updated. Although many people will complain about code compliances, they are made into law to assist in people's safety. For example, I've experienced a church placing more than fifty youth on a second floor. When we began renovation of that particular area, we discovered that the floor joists were sagging nearly two inches. The church was literally moments away from a structural failure and a huge blow to their ministry. Over the years, many church members had unknowingly cut holes in the floor joists in improper locations and improper sizes, which caused structural integrity problems. Thank goodness we were able to fix the issue before it was a problem—or before anybody was fatally injured.

One church I renovated had two ceilings in the fellowship hall. The lower ceiling had covered up the original ceiling, which had exposed wires and open junction boxes. When the lower ceiling was torn out, I noticed where an electrical fire had started in two places. Thankfully, it had not continued and did not burn down the building.

I have seen children put in a basement for their classes without the proper number of exits. These children were in danger if a fire were ever to occur. I also have experienced a lack of security in preschool and children areas, where anyone could grab a child and exit the facility before being stopped. Additionally, I've been in churches that did not have proper lock-down procedures or fire drills/plans in place.

On the other hand, I've seen many great ministries invest in those yet to come. Preschool and children's ministries are updated to provide a safe, clean environment. One church built the proper connect space and worship center, only to have one hundred and twenty-eight people give their lives to Christ on dedication Sunday. Another church baptized fifty-eight people during the second Sunday in a new worship facility. God honored their obedience to step out on faith and provide a place to facilitate growth.

Our facilities need to provide accessibility for all handicaps and physical impairments. Many times people naturally think about wheelchairs, but they forget those who are blind or hearing impaired or use crutches or canes. It is also necessary to think about providing spaces for other ministries, such as special-needs children.

Lastly, think of each space in your church as adaptable and usable for multiple ministries. The more flexible you can make spaces, the more ministries you can carry out in less space, which makes for good stewardship.

The natural synergy between your building and outward

focus is evident by having the tools to minister to others by meeting their needs. When we provide facilities that are open to serve and minister to the community, we become a healthier church.

10 HEALTHY CHURCHES VERSUS UNHEALTHY CHURCHES

The following is a summary of comparisons from my own observations as I've worked with hundreds of churches throughout the United States. I gathered further insights from Dr. Richard J. Krejcir's research he completed from 1998 to 2007 through the Francis A. Schaeffer Institute of Church Leadership Development.[15] I have listed my personal observations that coincide with the trends Dr. Krejcir discovered.

- Healthy churches have a first impression team constantly working on improving the first two to three visits. Unhealthy churches have facility teams focused on improving their facilities for their members.
- Healthy churches strongly encourage their members

to read the Bible daily. Unhealthy churches neglect the personal discipleship of their members.
- Healthy churches have a strong emphasis on groups, including Sunday school, life groups, home groups, and community groups. Unhealthy churches are focused on large group worship only and see little attendance in small groups.
- Healthy churches take care of their facilities, clean up the clutter, and look like they are expecting company. Unhealthy churches neglect maintenance and ignore areas that desperately need repair.
- Healthy churches focus on quality preschool and children spaces. Unhealthy churches are not concerned with young families because they give the least to the budget.
- Healthy churches are good at moving worship attenders to small group discipleship or to service on ministry teams. Unhealthy churches only focus on worship attendance.
- Healthy churches are constantly improving accessibility to all spaces. Unhealthy churches have a maze of different elevation changes throughout the campus.
- Healthy churches are outwardly focused on ways they can reach their communities, minister to their needs, and disciple them. Unhealthy churches are inwardly

focused: the highest priorities are the ways it has always been done and that which makes them the most comfortable.
- Healthy churches are part of and reflect their communities. Unhealthy churches are unwilling to look like the community or to change ethnically, age-related, or socioeconomically.
- Healthy churches have leaders who surrender to the lordship of Christ and build their churches on His foundation. Unhealthy churches tend to have leadership who are prideful and build their churches on the foundation of their legacies or personalities.
- Healthy churches are focused on prayer—for their communities, for the lost, and for God to work through them and in them. Unhealthy churches tend not to be focused on prayer, seeking what they desire and ignoring what God and His Word has for them.
- Healthy churches are in line with and in touch with Jesus Christ as Savior and Lord and understand is God at work in believers' lives. They seek His presence out of gratitude for who He is and what He has done. Unhealthy churches tend to be places of social status where the leadership is in control for personal agendas and/or are seeking trends contrary to the agenda or call of God's Word.

- Healthy churches have pastors and leaders who are humble, exhibit the fruit of the Spirit, and have a strong sense of indebtedness to God and others. Unhealthy churches tend to have pastors and leaders who are not humble but rather seek formulas and trends and do not feel indebtedness to God and/or others.
- Healthy churches place God's priorities first. Unhealthy churches only desire to produce what the leaders want.
- Healthy churches have leaders who do personal devotions and for whom the study of God's Word is the foundation of their faith and practice. Their "backstage" is healthy. Unhealthy churches tend to have leaders who do little or no little personal devotions and negate the study of God's Word.
- Healthy churches have a strong sense of biblical value for faith in the practice of church and personal life. The Bible is real and relevant in the lives of their leaders, so it is taught as well as caught from one another. Unhealthy churches tend to have a weak sense of biblical worth and see faith as just personal, not practiced in the life of the church. The Bible is seen as unrelated to church leadership, and thus they seek substitutes from nonbiblical or psychological/cultural sources.
- Healthy churches encourage people to know and exercise their spiritual gifts, and the strongest churches

mentor their people in them. Unhealthy churches tend to ignore its people's gifting and talents.

- Healthy churches are making disciples for the transformation of the whole person, both in faith and personal life. Unhealthy churches tend not to be interested in making disciples, and thus its people experience little or no sanctification in their personal lives.
- Healthy churches have pastors and leaders who are equipping others to serve, doing so with care and kindness; they see their people as participants in the ministries of their churches. Unhealthy churches tend to see their people as consumers, not participants.
- Healthy churches have leaders who are trained and get involved in the life of their churches. Unhealthy churches tend to have leaders who are not involved in the people's lives or the life of the church—unless it centers on them.
- Healthy churches see all their ministries and ministry teams as meaningful and important, and the people in them feel supported, encouraged, and equipped. Unhealthy churches tend to see a pecking order in ministries where one or two get all the attention and the rest are ignored.
- Healthy churches have a collective mindset of being a place of faithful character and practicing joyful fellowship. Unhealthy churches tend to have a collective

mindset of being a place where there is a lack of intention of warmth, of learning, of being faithful, and the practice of joyful fellowship is absent.

- Healthy churches have and emphasize small groups and/or Bible studies, equip and train their leaders, and offer quality curriculum fitting the spiritual developmental level of the participants. Unhealthy churches tend not to emphasize small groups or Bible studies, and if they do have them, they do not equip and train their leaders, nor do they offer quality curriculum for the spiritual developmental of the participants.
- Healthy churches have worship services where God's presence is sought and felt and the service alive with energy. The congregation feels inspired and fed. Also, there is a strong sense of God as the pastors and leaders facilitate worship. (Style and tradition are not significant factors; passion and prayer are.) Unhealthy churches tend to have worship services that are perfunctory, dull, dry, and where God's presence is not felt. There is a strong sense that the leader is performing to the audience of the church members.
- Healthy churches have clarity of vision and purpose and are also able to live it and communicate it to their church people. The people know what their churches are about and feel a part of and connected in them. Unhealthy

churches tend not to have clarity of vision or purpose and, if they do, do not follow it (or only a few do) or communicate it to their church people. The people have no idea what their churches' functions are and do not feel connected in them.

- Healthy churches are making disciples and serving their communities and the world. Those who go into missions or ministry come from being mentored and discipled. Unhealthy churches tend not to make disciples and thus have few (or no one) people serving or preparing to serve their communities and the world.
- Healthy churches are forgiving and see people in need of love and care; they have a sense of other people as God's children, too. Unhealthy churches tend not to recognize other people as God's children and are unforgiving. (Most people leave a church because of conflict.)
- Healthy churches are stewardship focused, teaching and encouraging their people to give out of their time, talents, and treasures. They are not forced or manipulated; rather, they freely give out of gratitude to the Lord for the mission of the church. Unhealthy churches tend to skew what stewardship is about and either ignore it or manipulate their people to give. (Real giving is always out of a grateful and generous heart, not out of obligation or manipulation.)

- Healthy churches are outwardly focused. They seek ways to reach out to people and train their people to do so both locally and globally. They see the entire world as the mission. Unhealthy churches tend to be inwardly focused and do not have outreach and/or mission programs, or only a few know about it and are involved in it. They see their churches as only reaching out to their "own kind" and rarely or only superficially go beyond their own church memberships. They see themselves as the mission.
- Healthy churches care about their people and programs and seek how they can improve what they are there to learn and do; they do not compare themselves to other churches. Unhealthy churches tend not to care about their people, nor do they seek improvement; there is a disregard for what they are there for, and they love to compare themselves to other churches.
- Healthy churches are concerned with strategic planning and being good stewards with their resources. They realize marketing is not about programs but about being a good model and witness. Unhealthy churches tend to do little strategic planning and/or are overconfident about marketing techniques and trends; they also do not use their resources wisely or effectively.
- Healthy churches measure success by how they are

impacting life changes in others' lives; it is quality over quantity. Unhealthy churches tend to measure success solely by numbers and desire quantity over quality.

- Healthy churches have facilities that are well cared for, clean, and usable. They see their churches as gathering points and tools for use by God and His people. Unhealthy churches also tend to have facilities that are well cared for and clean. But their facilities tend not to be usable; they see their churches as ministries to themselves and not to be messed up; thus, they are not used. Church facilities that are dilapidated, dirty, and unsanitary tend to be that way in worship and ministry as well.

- Healthy churches have more than 70 percent of their church members in Bible studies or small groups. In these small groups, the main curriculum is the Bible. Unhealthy churches have little to no active participation in small groups, and/or the groups are using weak curriculum that does not teach or inform about biblical principles, and the Bible is used very little.

I'm confident that if you are reading this book, then you are a pastor or lay leader who wants to see your church continue to become a healthier, more vibrant, and growing ministry. These simple conclusions are strong indicators that I see every day in churches we are working with. It is an interesting fact that regardless of the denomination, location, or size of churches, these healthy and unhealthy trends remain consistent. I strongly encourage you to review each of the above areas and prayerfully determine what areas are healthy and unhealthy in your ministry. The next step is to build a coalition for the change you need instituted, then take a step in faith and trust God to give you wisdom, favor, and strength to complete the work He has begun. You can do it. The best is yet to come.

11 ADVICE TO PASTORS AND LEADERS ENTERING A BUILDING PROGRAM

When I meet for the first time with pastors on new church projects, I offer advice to the church staff and the building team directly from Scripture. I would also like to offer this same information to you in hopes that I can be Barnabas to you, encouraging you with the Word. I would also like to offer a few recommendations for the process.

When you decide to step out and do anything great for God, the enemy does not like it. When you enter into the realm of a building program, you are entering the realm of spiritual warfare as much as any other area of your ministry. This is certainly not to discourage you but to prepare you. Remember, "Greater is He who is in you, than he who is in this world" (1 John 4:4 NASB).

You are about to embark on a journey that creates a tool for your ministry to evangelize the lost, disciple the saved, and serve the community. You are building an impact center, a hub for the community, a home for God's children, and a place where God's family can come and worship Him, love one another, and meet needs. This is a place where the Holy Spirit can heal the sick, convict sinners, and encourage us to stand, persevere, and move forward in our relationships with Christ. Yes, God can work in other places, no doubt. But this place is holy ground.

Therefore, don't be surprised when the enemy does not like what is about to happen. I have found that any existing problem in the church is magnified during a building program. So, it is time to get your house in order. Any issues of unity, pride, financial stress, clarity, personnel, and especially any morality issues in the leadership (lay or staff) must be resolved quickly and completely before moving forward.

A good leader knows how to get in the presence of God, knows His heart, and knows how to influence and build his team. A team of leaders can do so much more than one leader himself. A successful building project begins with a leader who builds excellent teams.

This battle to protect your ministry must be fought on the spiritual front. I encourage you to study the books of Ezra, Nehemiah, and Haggai, where you will find incredible insight from God in regards to what to expect during a building program. God has given us incredible examples of what can happen, how people can act, how to lead, and His sovereignty during a building program. For a great study on Nehemiah, I highly recommend writings on this topic by Dr. O. S. Hawkins.

When God tells us to build His house, He will always provide godly leadership. God used a team of godly men to lead His people back from seventy years of captivity to Jerusalem to rebuild the temple and the walls of Jerusalem. Zerubbabel, Jeshua, Ezra, Nehemiah, Haggai, and Zechariah were men called to obey and to lead. God also turned other men's hearts to accomplish His will, including King Cyrus, King Darius, and King Artaxerxes.

GET IN THE WORD AND SEEK HIS FACE

First and foremost, you must get back to the basics. God tells us in Hosea 10:12 to "sow with a view to righteousness, reap in accordance with kindness; break up your fallow ground, for it is time to seek the Lord until He comes to rain righteousness on you" (NASB). Like never before, seek His face and get in His Word. The Hebrew word used in the Old

Testament when discussing the Sabbath is *Shabbot*, which means "to cease, stop, and spend time with Him." In Ezra 3, when Zerubbabel and Jeshua arrived in Jerusalem, they first built an altar to God and offered burnt offerings before celebrating the Feast of Booths. They got back to the basics of worshiping God before rebuilding the temple.

As you begin your process, first evaluate honestly your situation and face the problems honestly. You must have the strength, patience, wisdom, and understanding to do something about it. Trust God to work through your circumstances and specific situation. Look at the example given to us in Nehemiah. When he heard of the condition of Jerusalem, he fasted and prayed before God. In Ezra 7:9–10 we learn why God's favor was upon Ezra: "Because the good hand of his God was upon him. For Ezra had set his heart to study the law of the Lord and to practice it, and to teach His statutes and ordinances in Israel" (NASB). Ezra had the favor of God because he was in the Word, obeyed the Word, lived the Word, and taught the Word.

After you seek God, you must identify your needs, take personal responsibility, move out of your comfort zone, and take action. Carefully assess your current situation, then move forward with focus on conceivable, believable, and achievable goals.

Satan would love to distract you from keeping the

main thing the main thing by distracting you with numerous challenges, such as raising money, dealing with problems among your people, creating buy-in or ownership for the vision, determining what to build and what your priorities and personal preferences are, and/or dealing with past experiences or rumors of building project experiences. Keep the focus of the church about growing, serving, and reaching people for Christ. As O. S. Hawkins put it, your opposition will come through "derision, danger, discouragement, and distraction."[16]

You will have a crisis or some form of distraction during the process. We see the people of the land discouraging the people of Judah in Ezra 4, frightening them and even hiring counselors to make false claims against the king to frustrate their plans. This delayed work for sixteen years. They were convinced it was the wrong time to build (ever heard that before?). The economy is bad; it's the wrong time; we're fatigued. God then used Haggai and Zechariah to tell the people they it *is* time to rebuild the temple. The Lord reminded them that is was wrong for them to live in luxury houses while the temple lay in ruins and urged them to consider the consequences of their indifference. They wanted their wealth for themselves, not a temple. Like many of us, they weren't thinking about the children who would hear the gospel because of the building program, the youth who would be saved from a life of drugs, and the marriages that would be restored and saved from divorce, all because a tool was provided to grow, serve, and reach people.

In Nehemiah, distractions included Sanballat, Tobiah, and Geshem mocking them, threatening a military attack, trying to lure Nehemiah outside of Jerusalem, bringing false charges against Nehemiah, paying his friend to provide a false prophecy to discredit Nehemiah, and then bringing in spies to Jerusalem to frighten and threaten him. In the middle of all that, the people got upset at each other about working so hard, being drained financially, and being so burdened by taxes that they had to hire out their wives and children.[19]

Remember to set clear objectives with specific needs. Pick the right person for the right job. The truth is, anytime someone takes God at His word and begins to build something of value, there will be a Sanballat, Tobiah, or Geshem to mock, ridicule, and attack morale, motive, and mission.

Nehemiah led by example by lending money without interest and releasing people of their debts. He never took his eyes off of what God called him to do: "I am doing a great work and I cannot come down" (NASB). He knew why he was building the temple and the source of strength and provision: "When I saw their fear, I rose and spoke to the nobles, the officials and the rest of the people: 'Do not be afraid of them; remember the Lord who is great and awesome, and fight for your brothers, your sons, your daughters, your wives, and your houses'" (Nehemiah 4:14 NASB).

When your building is completed, you will know that God did it. Keep doing what is right. Rally the troops. Remain faithful. Finish strong. Give glory to God. God did it! Nehemiah 6:16 says, "When all our enemies heard of it, and all the nations surrounding us saw it, they lost their confidence; for they recognized that this work had been accomplished with the help of our God" (NASB).

PROTECTING YOUR MINISTRY DURING A BUILDING PROGRAM

1. SET YOUR EXPECTATIONS CORRECTLY.

There is no such thing as a perfect set of plans or a construction project without problems. It is how you and your professional handle the problems that make a difference. When a crisis hits, respond quickly, generously, and gently.

This process can be an emotional roller coaster. You may not even like the process at times. Understand that building programs usually cost more and take longer than you want. Remember, this is a process of give and take, not an event. You will be constantly making decisions to maximize the ministry return on your investment.

Honestly assess where you are. Study your growth patterns, counting heads not eyeballs. Is your ministry healthy and balanced? Where is it out of balance? What are your needs, not just wants and wishes?

Again, Ezra, Nehemiah, and Haggai offer many parallels of what you can expect during a building program. These books touch on:

- how to prepare;
- how to celebrate victories;
- what not to do that will stop the program;
- how to deal with resistance from the enemy inside and outside the church;
- how to stay focused on God's vision and trust Him; and
- how to give God all the glory when it is done.

The bottom line is that you need to get your house in order right now. Any problem that exists in your ministry—people, leadership, or team unity—will be magnified several times during a building program.

Expect the enemy to show up. Anytime you step out to do something great for God, the enemy will rear his head, and a building program is no different. Remember, God loves you, Jesus is Lord, and we have victory!

2. PREPARE SPIRITUALLY.

The first thing God's people did when they returned to a desolate Jerusalem after seventy years of Babylonian captivity was reestablish the sacrifices and celebrate the Festival of Booths. In essence, they got back to the basics of connecting with God. Like the Israelites, you must keep the main thing the main thing.

I highly recommend Thom Rainer's book, *Who Moved My Pulpit*, to provide simple solutions to lead change in your church. Preparing spiritually for change is exactly the same as preparing for your building program.

- *Stop and pray.* Nehemiah 1:4 says, "When I heard these words, I sat down and wept. I mourned for a number of days, fasting and praying before the God of heaven."
- *Pray for God's wisdom.* You are facing a spiritual battle with critics and naysayers. You are asking God to lead you through this unknown future. (See James 1:5.)
- *Pray for God's courage.* There will be days when you wonder if it is worth it. Change can be difficult. (See 2

Timothy 1:7.)
- *Pray for God's strength.* (See Isaiah 40:29–31). Leading your church through a building program without prayer will not work, nor is it wise. As Thom Rainer notes in *Who Moved My Pulpit*, "I have never seen successful and sustaining change take place in a church without prayer. Never. Not once."
- *Remember what got you to the point of needing to build.* Put on the full armor of God daily. Remember the spiritual disciplines that keep you connected and walking in the Spirit. Stay outwardly focused; you are doing this to "go and make disciples."

Become a student of healthy church growth. There are great resources available to help you discover how to create a healthy, balanced ministry.

Shabbat. Cease. Stop. Take a little Sabbath. You must revive, restore, and recharge yourself. On a regular basis, "Be still, and know that I am God" (Psalm 46:10 NIV). Take time to enjoy life and enjoy time with your Lord. Don't neglect your family or your health. Appreciate the journey. Relax—it's God's work. God's work, done God's way, never lacks God's blessing.

Don't forget that your ministry also involves the relationship with your professional. Develop a culture of trust and transparency with your designer/builder. Additionally, you will have the opportunity to minister to numerous people who will be part of your project who may otherwise never step foot into your church. Love the workers, share the gospel, and watch them get saved or grow in their faith, work harder for you, and finish the project strong.

3. PRIORITIZE YOUR MINISTRY NEEDS.

This begins with developing a dynamic strategic master plan. It is dynamic because it must be ever-changing and flexible. It is strategic because you are moving in a specific direction. It is a plan indicating that you are going to be a wise steward of what the Lord has given you. Motivation, momentum, and morale are often shaped by clear vision and direction. This is one of the most important parts of the project and the least expensive. Take your time and get this right.

Your designer must first understand your ministry and then wrap your building around it, rather than trying to fit your ministry into a building. I recommend beginning this process by meeting with each ministry team to understand their needs fully. Begin by understanding the good, the bad, the ugly. Discuss where each area of ministry is strong, weak, and its issues. The meetings should include brainstorming everything you think is needed to grow the ministry. Then prioritize those needs in each ministry by listing them in order.

Always keep your ministry in mind. As Winston Churchill said, "We shape our buildings; thereafter they shape us."[17]

After this, the leadership team should prioritize the needs of the entire ministry. Take the various ministry needs and determine what is most important to provide a healthy ministry. Identify what part of your ministry is most out of balance. This will likely be the area that is most hindering your growth.

Remember to consider first impressions: the website, parking, welcome and greeting, preschool and children ministry, youth ministry, worship quality, sermons, connect commons space, small group space, tithe and offering, closing, bathrooms, signage, and outreach. Consider how each of these areas communicates to a first-time guest.

Ensure that executing your planned project will protect your ministry during construction. Protect your people from the hazards of construction in every way possible. Sure, there will be inconveniences; however, make sure that the construction sequence will not destroy your ministry in the process of building.

4. PREPARE FINANCIALLY.

The worst thing you could do is take on so much debt that you put your ministry in a financial pickle. Study your finances with the understanding you cannot take on so much debt that it will prevent you from being able to minister effectively.

Determine how much discretionary income you can direct to debt service. You need to build the debt service into your current operating budget and pay yourself that amount (savings) every month. This will do several things:

- increase your cash into the project;
- reduce your total principle of debt;
- show you and your team that you can handle that debt service and not adversely affect ministry;
- allow everything you raise to go against the loan principle; and
- get you better lender terms and conditions because you demonstrated your ability to handle the loan.

5. BUILD EXCELLENT TEAMS.

A successful building project begins with a leader who builds an excellent team. Rainer explained that in order to build an excellent team, an eager coalition for the church project must first be built. This is where most leaders fail. It takes a lot of time and patience to get a team of key people to buy in to the vision. These people need to have good chemistry with you, hold key positions in the church, and have the influence and expertise to back your vision.

First, the process is usually informal. Meet with key people over a meal, coffee, or in the office, where you can present the idea and spend time listening and receiving input from that key person.

Second, the process is individual. This step is usually a one-on-one meeting to ensure clear communication.

Third, the process can be lengthy. The bigger the change and project, the more time it may take to get complete understanding and buy in. Typically, short-term leaders take more time to build the coalition than longer-term leaders.

Keep your building team small. If you have more than five to seven people on your decision-making team, you will have a lot of lengthy discussions and could become frustrated by the inability to make decisions quickly. These people need to have a heart for and understanding of the ministry, more than merely the knowledge of design, construction, or financing. You are hiring a professional with expertise in church design and construction who exhibits a track record of integrity. Put people on your team who can understand, communicate, and live out the vision.

6. BE A LEADER OF HOPE AND VISION.

Rainer explained that when leading change, in spite of all the critics and multiple issues in the church, you must be the voice of constant vision and hope. I have never seen a successful building program where the lead pastor was not sold out to the vision and had confidence that God was leading them in that direction.

Rainer recommends several Scriptures:

- Psalm 38:15
- Psalm 62:5
- Psalm 147:11
- Lamentations 3:24
- Acts 26:6
- 2 Corinthians 3:12
- Hebrews 10:23

A healthy church has a hopeful and visionary pastor. Three traits of leaders who embody hope are:

- They read the Bible daily.
- They choose to communicate hope in all communications.
- They look for low-hanging fruit. Find small wins to build momentum and celebrate the victories.

7. WORK HARD TO COMMUNICATE WITH YOUR CHURCH.

You will want to develop momentum along the way by sharing the top three things you are excited about that just happened in the process. This needs to happen at least monthly. This needs to be done as a testimony from a layperson and staff members who have influence and respect from the congregation. These things can be small like:

- "I'm excited that your leadership is taking the time to study our financial positions and make sure we are being good stewards of resources."
- "I'm excited that our leadership team is working diligently to take care of the needs of our young families by looking at ways to give them the best tool for their ministry."

- "I'm confident that our leadership is exploring all ways to make accessibility for our senior saints a priority."

These testimonies need to be authentic and passionate. Do not present information to the congregation until you are 100 percent sure you are moving in that direction. Your team must prevent leaks of information of costs, space allocation, or renderings of the building until you are confident and unified on the direction. This will save many headaches and much confusion.

As you develop the next phase site and floor plans, renderings, and budgets, make sure to put the vision in front of the people in as many ways as possible. Share in small group spaces. Place pictures in high traffic areas of the campus. Place material on the website and social media. Don't forget to communicate to the community that you are building for those yet to come.

RECOMMENDED RESOURCES

I recommend the following resources if you are entering a building program:

- *I Am a Church Member* by Thom Rainer
- *Change Your Space, Change Your Culture* by Rex Miller
- *Who Moved My Pulpit* by Thom Rainer
- *Autopsy of a Deceased Church* by Thom Rainer
- *The Advantage* by Patrick Lencioni
- *The Ideal Team Player* by Patrick Lencioni
- *Simple Church* by Eric Geiger
- *Good to Great* by Jim Collins
- *Replenish* by Lance Witt
- *Leading on Empty* by Wayne Cordeiro
- *The Unstuck Church* by Tony Morgan
- *Comeback Churches* by Stetzer & Dodson

12 RECOMMENDATIONS FOR THOSE WHO CANNOT BUILD NOW

Your church may not be ready to build. Perhaps you don't have the budget for a renovation or expansion. Perhaps you don't feel like the timing is right to move the congregation toward a building project. If your church is not in the position to move forward, let me suggest how to improve your facility without spending lots of money. I also recommend you review the First Impressions sections in Chapter 3.

Prepare yourself now to become the pastor or ministry team that can handle the blessings of more people, expanded ministries, and opportunities with excellence. Think of these things:

- Prepare for guests.
- Look like you are expecting company.

- Whatever you do, do it with excellence, as unto the Lord.
- Maximize the use of your existing facilities, keeping them clean, safe, and a ministry tool, not a sacred cow.
- Find a mentor who has been where you are and has moved where you want to be.
- Use an anonymous guest survey to see how you are doing at least once a year.
- Become a student of church health. I recommend joining with a church health expert leader like Thom Rainer at ChurchAnswers.com or RevitalizedChurches.com.
- Develop your leaders to be disciple makers.
- Read the Bible every day.
- Lead your church members to read their Bibles every day, and they will be more likely to evangelize, minister to the community, pray, give, and become a unifying force in the church.

ACKNOWLEDGMENTS

I was blessed to grow up in a Christian home where I had a father and mother who took—not sent—me to church. I saw them reading the Bible on a regular basis, serving in ministries at our church, teaching Sunday school, leading youth group, serving as a deacon and elder, preaching at times to fill in for the pastor, and working diligently at our church camp, both in season and out of season. I remember asking why they bought a station wagon when we did not need one (nor did us three boys want one), and they said if they did not pick up some youth for church, they would not go to church, so we needed the extra room. I observed my parents tithe faithfully. I experienced my parents love each other and stay committed to their family and marriage (for more than fifty-three years). I saw them love God, give faithfully, and serve where and whenever needed. Is it really any wonder that at the young age of seven I committed my life to Christ and followed their footsteps?

Thank you, Mom and Dad, for being the example, teaching me about the greatest gift we could ever have, and staying committed to Christ, each other, and our family. I thank God for blessing me with an incredible example. You were an example of God's love until I could understand His incredible love personally.

I want to thank my Proverbs 31 wife, Cheryl, for her encouragement in everything in life. During every victory and every storm, she has stood by my side. When I felt led to help pastors and their building teams understand critical aspects of the design and construction process that would make their building experiences a blessing and not a curse, she encouraged me to write a book. Next to my salvation in Christ, Cheryl has been God's greatest gift in my life. She is an incredible wife, mother, business partner, and friend.

ABOUT THE AUTHOR

Tim is a top graduate of the United States Air Force Academy in Aeronautical Engineering and an Academic All-American for swimming and diving. On an NCAA athletic scholarship, Tim earned a master's degree in Aerospace Engineering from the University of Kansas. After serving as an officer in the USAF and flying developmental and operational flight test missions for various aircraft while also owning and operating a few small businesses, Tim accepted the call to the ministry to help churches with professional capital stewardship campaigns as a partner, coach, enabler, equipper, and motivator. He was also involved with financial planning, estate planning, and church financing consultation.

In 2000 Tim joined COSCO & Associates, Inc., a national firm that specializes in church design, construction, sales, and marketing. In 2001 Tim separated from the USAF and joined the COSCO team full time as vice president of operations. He became a student of the industry and began obtaining his licensing as a general contractor in numerous states. He was promoted to president of COSCO in 2003.

The Lord has given Tim a heart for the process of church growth and development. He recognizes that it is building a ministry, not just a facility.

Tim is ordained in ministry and often preaches at the churches he is working with throughout the country. He is a member of Woodlawn Baptist Church. He serves as an adult couples Sunday school teacher and has served in numerous capacities in the other churches he has attended, from deacon, to greeter, to preschool worker, to working with children in AWANA, to working with the youth group, along with many leadership teams. He enjoys flying, motocross and ATVs, golfing, skiing, triathlons, and spending time with his family. Tim, his wife, Cheryl, and his son, John, reside in Crestview, Florida. Their son, Rick, and his wife Dominque, serve in the USAF.

END NOTES

1. Rick Warren, "Forget Church Growth, Aim for Church Health", *Pastors.com*, May 16, 2016, http://pastors.com/health-not-growth/.
2. Ibid.
3. Ibid.
4. Warren, "Forget Church Growth".
5. Warren Wiersbe, as quoted in Joe McKeever, "Balance: The Key to a Healthy Church", *Ministry Today*, January 1, 2015, http://ministrytodaymag.com/leadership/vision/21486-balance-the-key-to-a-healthy-church.
6. Warren, "Forget Church Growth".
7. Ibid.
8. Thom Rainer, *I Am a Church Member: Discovering the Attitude that Makes a Difference* (Nashville, TN: B & H, 2013).
9. Ibid.
10. Thom Rainer, *Autopsy of a Deceased Church: 12 Ways to*

Keep Yours Alive (Nashville, TN: B & H, 2014).

11. Ibid.

12. Alan Taylor, Men's Conference, FBC Woodstock, Woodstock, GA, March 2006.

13. Tony Morgan, *Vital Signs: Meaningful Metrics That Keep a Pulse on Your Church's Health* (The Unstuck Group, 2014).

14. Oswald Chambers, *Prayer: A Holy Occupation* (Grand Rapids MI: Discovery House, 1992), 111.

15. R. J. Krejcir, Ph.D., *Francis A. Schaeffer Institute of Church Leadership Development,* www.churchleadership.org.

16. Dr. O.S. Hawkins, "Rebuilding: Rebuilders never cut what they can untie—Part 5", *OSHawkins.com*, http://www.oshawkins.com/sermons/rebuilders-never-cut-what-they-can-untie/.

17. Winston Churchill, (1874–1965), cited in: Randal O'Toole *The Best-Laid Plans* (Washington, D. C., Cato Institute, 2007), 161.

18. Marshall McLuhan, *The Medium is the Message* (repr., Cambridge, MA: Massachusetts Institute of Technology Press, 1994).

19. Terry Trivette, "Overcoming Opposition", *Standandspeak.org* (Covington Theological Seminary, 2010).

Made in the USA
Middletown, DE
12 November 2018